# License to Laugh

# LICENSE TO LAUGH

## Humor in the Classroom

Richard A. Shade

1996
**Teacher Ideas Press**
A Member of
Greenwood Publishing
88 Post Road West
Westport, Connecticut

*In memory of Dodie Shade—*
*Keep your wonderful sense of humor Mom!*

◆

TEACHERS IDEA PRESS
A Member of
Greenwood Publishing
88 Post Road West
Westport, Connecticut

*Production Editor:* Kevin W. Perizzolo
*Copy Editor:* Jason Cook
*Proofreader:* Susie Sigman
*Typesetter:* Kay Minnis

**Library of Congress Cataloging-in-Publication Data**

Shade, Richard A., 1954-
    License to laugh : humor in the classroom / by Richard A. Shade.
    xviii, 127 p. 17x25 cm.
    Includes bibliographical references (p. 119) and index.
    ISBN 1-56308-364-7
    1. Teaching. 2. Humor in education. 3. Teacher-student
relationships. I. Title.
LB1027.S4655        1996
371.1'02'0207--dc20                                     96-20533
    P                                                       CIP

In order to keep this title in print and available to the academic community, this edition
was produced using digital reprint technology in a relatively short print run. This would
not have been attainable using traditional methods. Although the cover has been changed
from its original appearance, the text remains the same and all materials and methods
used still conform to the highest book-making standards.

# Contents

# Preface

In writing *License to Laugh: Humor in the Classroom*, it is my intention to help teachers bridge the gap between theory and practice and encourage them to be more aware of and sensitive to the powerful role appropriate humor plays in the teaching and learning process. To this end, I have provided background related literature and materials designed to present to the reader both a broad view and a comprehensive look at this rather complex and sophisticated topic. I have addressed various aspects related to the theoretical, historical, developmental, and contemporary perspectives of humor.

The use of humor in the classroom as a teaching and learning tool is a relatively new area of study among researchers and educators and is filled with fragmentary knowledge about its benefits. The carefully chosen references, although appearing somewhat dated, are seminal in nature and importance.

Designed with both preservice and inservice teachers in mind, this book includes over one hundred classroom-tested activities! Activities you can begin to use in your classroom the first thing Monday morning! Activities that work!

Enjoy!

— Richard A. Shade

# Acknowledgments

The author wishes to extend thanks and appreciation to the following individuals:

- ◆ Dr. Tracy Cross for his collegial support and friendship over the years as we have explored various topics and aspects of humor. (Thank you, thank you very much!)

- ◆ Dr. Ace Cossairt for his expertise as we developed and delivered humor workshops and institutes for teachers.

- ◆ Mary Alice Bruce for unwavering, constant kindness; your overwhelming understanding.

- ◆ To the many learners I have had the pleasure to encounter in my public school and university teaching experiences.

Finally, the author wishes to express great thanks to all the editors and support personnel at Libraries Unlimited and Teacher Ideas Press for their continued support and guidance.

# Introduction

Humor is all around us! All we have to do is—Stop! Look! Listen! Humor is certainly ever present in the classroom. Whether you teach preschool students, college students, or any grade level in-between, you have probably found yourself in situations resembling these:

## ➤ Preschool/Kindergarten

Missy: I won a prize in kindergarten today! Teacher asked me how many legs a hippopotamus has, and I said "three."
Dad: Three. How on earth could you have won the prize?
Missy: My teacher said I came the closest.

Two first graders were standing outside the school one morning:

Chris: Do you think thermonuclear projectiles would pierce the sound barrier?
Carl: No, once a force enters the substratosphere . . .

Then the recess bell rang.

Chris: There goes the bell. Now we have to go inside and string beads. ◄

## ➤ Elementary School

Teacher: Yes, Brian, what is it?
Brian: I don't want to scare you, but my dad said if I didn't get better grades, someone is due for a spanking! ◄

## ➤ Junior High School

Sammy came to school with a bloody nose and swollen eyes:

Teacher: You've been fighting again! Didn't I tell you to count to 50 before you fought with anyone?
Sammy: Yes, but someone told Bill to only count to 25! ◄

## ➤ High School

The day before a lunar eclipse, the teacher announced to his class that they should be sure to watch the total eclipse at 9:00 p.m. the following evening:

Teacher: This is one of the most wonderful shows that nature will ever offer you, and it's free for all to enjoy.
Eric: What channel will it be on? ◄

## ➤ College

A professor at a medical school asked a student how much of a certain drug should be administered to a patient:

Student: I believe five grains.

The professor went on with the lecture. A minute later the young medical student raised his hand:

Student: Professor, I would like to change my answer to that question.

The professor glanced at his watch.

Professor: Never mind, young man, your patient has been dead for 40 seconds! ◄

Although you may not think each of these examples uproariously funny, you can appreciate and comprehend this humor because you can relate to these experiences and this school setting. Appreciation and comprehension are two of the elements that comprise a sense of humor. If reading about these situations evokes laughter, grins, smiles, giggles, or chuckles, you demonstrate another element: mirth response. These elements, along with two others—identification (the ability to distinguish or recognize something as humorous) and production (the ability to create and deliver humorous stimuli)—make it possible for us to get a total picture of a sense of humor. You and your students can experience humor in positive and appropriate ways, often with desirable effects on the learning process.

## The Role of Humor in the Educational Setting

Certain segments of society, as well as tradition and individual personalities and preferences, often present barriers to the effective use of appropriate humor in the classroom. Only recently has the appreciation, comprehension, and production of students' humor been examined by educators as a teaching enhancement. These barriers, as well as caveats to follow and boundaries to establish when using humor in the classroom, will be discussed.

Society in general, and perhaps especially professionals in the education field, is not in agreement as to the role and value of humor. Humor has been viewed both as a hindrance and an advantage to classroom teaching and learning. Humor is often seen as a disruptive influence in the classroom, and it may be a sign of immaturity in the child who produces it. However, as an advocate of the use of appropriate humor in the classroom, I see two potential benefits: humor's positive influence on classroom climate and its positive, decided effect on the teaching and learning process.

Some teachers tend to react to humor in their classroom as a disruptive behavior. They try to discourage the act as well as the students producing it. Although some exceptions have been noted with individual teachers and students, this negative perspective appears to be the prevailing attitude toward humor in the classroom. In light of this general negative attitude, there should be an awareness of the positive aspects of using humor in any classroom.

## What Is a Sense of Humor?

So what is this thing called "a sense of humor"? What elements comprise it? How can it be assessed? How is it related to cognition? What are the various forms of humor? Is humor developmental? How does a child's sense of humor differ from an adult's? How is humor viewed in the classroom? Can we appropriately infuse humor into daily classroom instruction? To what end? For what purpose? Can we cultivate a sense of humor in ourselves and our students? Can we integrate humor successfully into sound instructional design? What to do, what to do? These questions and more will be addressed in the chapters that follow.

Appropriate humor can be employed and strategically infused into any classroom environment to facilitate the learning of any academic content. This book contains methods, strategies, techniques, and activities designed to:

◆ Make teaching more fun

◆ Develop self-esteem

◆ Motivate students

- ◆ Reduce stress
- ◆ Teach academic content
- ◆ Stimulate creativity
- ◆ Open closed minds
- ◆ Maintain attention
- ◆ Assess comprehension
- ◆ Enhance thinking
- ◆ Energize students
- ◆ AND MORE!!!

Five elements—humor identification, humor appreciation (perception), humor mirth response, humor comprehension, and humor production—provide the framework for this book. The activities presented are "classroom-tested" by either myself or teachers in my workshops. The benefits of using humor in the classroom, general suggestions for classroom use, warnings related to the negative uses of humor, and classroom-tested ideas, resources, and additional topics are included in the chapters that follow. As I often tell my preservice teachers, "Try it!"

This book is designed to help you understand humor in its many forms, how you can use it intentionally and appropriately to enhance your pedagogy, and how to realize and share its benefits with students of all ages. The analogy "License to Laugh" implies that with humor comes accountability. *License* is defined by *Webster's Dictionary* as "authority granted to do any act; to permit by grant of authority." We have licenses to drive motorized vehicles—with that license comes the responsibility of knowing the rules, guidelines, and consequences. The same is true with the use of humor in the classroom. There are rules, guidelines, and consequences.

That same license also provides us with benefits: The benefits of driving a car include the freedom to move from point A to point B quickly, economically, comfortably, and safely. The same is also true with the use of humor. Numerous benefits of humor use in your classroom will become evident if you allow yourself the license to use it.

So, Enjoy!

# 1

# Introducing the Five Elements Related to Humor

Frequently, an assumption is made that humor is the resulting behavior of some single factor. However, it appears more reasonable to assume that a number of causal factors exist in combination to elicit a humorous response or humorous behavior. These factors, or abilities, are discussed singularly. The varying degree to which an individual possesses and demonstrates each, along with the numerous permutations of interrelationships that exist, provide us with the notion that sense of humor is a very individualistic phenomenon. An individual's sense of humor is comprised of five elements: humor identification, humor appreciation, humor mirth response, humor comprehension, and humor production. This chapter expands the definition and understanding of these elements.

**Model of the Five Elements of Humor**

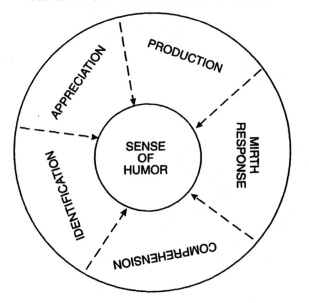

# Humor Identification

## The Four Forms of Humor

| FIGURAL | VERBAL |
|---|---|
| Comic books<br>Comic strips<br>Political Cartoons<br>Cartoons<br>Caricatures | Jokes<br>Puns<br>Riddles<br>Satire<br>Parody<br>Irony<br>Wit<br>Limerick<br>Anecdote |
| **VISUAL (Physical)** | **AUDITORY** |
| Impressions<br>Impersonations<br>Mime<br>Pantomime<br>Practical Jokes<br>Pratfalls<br>Slapstick<br>Sight Gags | Impressions<br>Impersonations<br>Noises<br>Sounds |

There are many different kinds of humor. However, humor can generally be placed into four distinct forms: figural, verbal, visual, and auditory.

## Figural Humor

Figural humor is commonly referred to as cartoons. Examples include cartoons, comic books, comic strips, political cartoons, and caricatures, all of which are often accompanied by captions. Cartoons can be single-panel, as in a political cartoon or a caricature, or sequenced, as in a comic strip.

◆ **Cartoons, Comic Books, and Comic Strips**—These employ illustrations to examine current news affairs, popular culture, mores, etc., in an amusing fashion. These artistic creations are usually presented in single- or multiple-panel formats. They often depict a serial story or a universal situation.

◆ **Political Cartoons**—Political cartoons differ from cartoons, comic books, and comic strips primarily in subject matter. They tell a politically related anecdote or story, or comment on a particular political character or issue, or on political life in general. Satire is often employed, and political cartoons often take the form of caricatures.

◆ **Caricatures**—These often involve a ludicrous exaggeration (usually in picture form) of peculiar personal characteristics. Caricatures are often line drawings, with at least one or two attributes of the subject distorted.

## Verbal Humor

Verbal humor has numerous forms, including but not limited to puns, riddles, jokes, satire, limericks, parody, anecdotes, farce, irony, sarcasm, tall tales, and wit. These require an ability in the reader or listener to comprehend language-based incongruities.

◆ **Pun**—The humorous use of a word so as to suggest a different meaning or application; a play on words. Sometimes a pun plays on words with the same or similar sound but different meaning. It has been said that it takes an intelligent person to create a pun, and a brave person to use one!

> Brian: Why does it take a runner longer to run from second to third base than from first to second base?
> Eric: Because there's a shortstop in between.

◆ **Riddle**—A word game; an enigma; a puzzling fact. A riddle, usually presented in a question-and-answer format, is similar in nature to a joke, but with a specific format.

> Matt: How do you keep fish from smelling?
> Jenny: Cut off their noses.

◆ **Joke**—Something said or done that provokes laughter. The source of this common form of humor can involve any or all of the following: comprehending the multiple meanings of words, idioms, and metaphors; discovering ambiguity; perceiving and ultimately comprehending the incongruity; and appreciating the unexpected or sudden change of perspective. When examining language-related humor, several different types of jokes become evident:

**Phonological**—based on the phonological structure of words.

> Rebecca: What is this?
> Waiter: It's bean soup.
> Rebecca: I don't care what it's "been." What is it now?

**Lexical**—based on multiple-meanings of words.

> Dave: What has 18 legs and catches flies?
> Lynn: A baseball team.

**Surface Structure**—based on the alternative grouping of words.

> Don: What kinds of flowers like to be kissed?
> Joan: A tulip (two lip).

**Deep Structure**—involves alternative interpretations of a word or phrase.

> Sue: What animal can jump higher than a house?
> Chris: Any animal. Houses can't jump.

**Metalinguistic**—focuses on the language form instead of the language meaning.

> Kathy: What's at the end of everything?
> Tim: The letter *g*.

These categories of jokes are evidence of the fact that students' cognitive, linguistic, and metalinguistic abilities are factors in their appreciation, comprehension, and production of jokes.

◆ **Satire**—A literary composition to ridicule vice or folly of the times; use of irony, sarcasm, invective, or wit. Satire often includes both humor and criticism. Techniques often involve exaggeration, distortion, and understatement.

> An old lady was sent on a 10-day cruise paid for by her son. She wrote to complain: "The food on this ship is absolutely awful. And such small portions!"

◆ **Limerick**—A five-lined nonsense verse (said to be from a song introducing the place name *Limerick).*

> There was a young lady called Bright
> Who could travel far faster than light;
> She set off one day,
> In a relative way,
> And returned home the previous night.

Although limericks are structured, writers sometimes "bend the rules" of traditional limerick format to produce amusing creations.

◆ **Parody**—An imitation of a poem, song, story, or movie, where the style is the same but the theme ludicrously different. Perhaps the "King of Parody" in songwriting, currently, is "Weird Al" Yankovic, with songs like "I Love Rocky Road" for "I Love Rock & Roll" and "Lasagna" for "La Bamba."

◆ **Anecdote**—An oral account (often entertaining) of a real or fictional event. Usually biographical, an anecdote involves the elaboration or embellishment of a story, occurrence, or event. Speakers often share anecdotes related to their work, their schooling, or something that happened on the way to a speaking engagement.

*Webster's Dictionary* defines anecdote as "a biographical incident; a brief account of any fact or happening (often amusing)." These entertaining accounts (often oral) are of real or fictitious events. Examples of anecdotes may be found in *Reader's Digest* in the "Humor in Uniform" and "Life in These United States" sections.

◆ **Farce**—A style of comedy marked by boisterous humor and extravagant gesture; absurd; ludicrous.

*Webster's Dictionary* defines farce as "a style of comedy marked by boisterous humor and extravagant gesture; absurd." A farce often makes fun of a particular event. An example, and one of my personal favorites, is a short film entitled "Hardware Wars." It is a spoof or farce of the *Star Wars Trilogy*. At one point in the film, the announcer even states, "May the *farce* (force) be with you."

◆ **Irony**—A mode of speech in which the intended meaning is the opposite of the literal meaning; sarcasm; satire.

*Webster's Dictionary* defines irony as "a mode of speech in which the meaning is the opposite of that actually expressed." An example of irony is when a severe snow storm forces you to cancel your planned ski vacation!

◆ **Sarcasm**—Taunt; scoffing gibe; veiled sneer; irony.

*Webster's Dictionary* defines sarcasm as "taunt; scoffing jibe; veiled sneer." An example would be if it was bitter cold outside and someone stated, "Hey, it's really cold outside!" And another person replied, "No—actually I'd really enjoy a snow cone to cool off right now."

◆ **Tall Tales**—Exaggeration is the key to the success of the tall tale. Most facts and events surrounding the characters, setting, and plots in the story range from the absurd to the impossible. The narrator tells the story as if it were true and factual to add to the humor of the situation (e.g., *Pecos Bill* and *Paul Bunyan*).

◆ **Wit**—Intellect; understanding; ingenuous connection of amusingly incongruous ideas; humor.

*Webster's Dictionary* defines wit as "(one with) ingenuity in connecting amusingly incongruous ideas; humor." Wit is often spontaneous, resulting in quick, "off the cuff" remarks. An example is:

Judge: "Order. Order in the courtroom."
Lawyer: "Okay. I guess I'll have a cheeseburger."

## Visual Humor

Visual humor includes slapstick, impersonations, mime or pantomime, facial gestures, pratfall, body language, and practical jokes. These are effective as one watches for some type of incongruity. Visual humor is synonymous with physical humor.

◆ **Slapstick**—Boisterous farce of pantomime or low comedy.

◆ **Impersonation**—To represent in character or form; to act a part on the stage; to imitate.

◆ **Mime/Pantomime**—A farce in which scenes of real life are expressed by gesture only.

◆ **Practical Joke** (includes pratfalls and visual sight gags)—Something said or done to provoke laughter; a prank.

## Auditory Humor

Auditory humor is associated exclusively with sounds and is a relatively small category. Perhaps one of the most classic examples would be from the television sitcom hit during the 1970s "All in the Family." Although we never saw the bathroom of the Bunker household, people eagerly anticipated the "toilet flush" associated with Archie Bunker. Other examples of auditory humor are various sound effects and imitations. Hence, these auditory forms of humor are not necessarily associated with words.

# Humor Appreciation

Humor appreciation is the second element related to humor. It is somewhat aligned with comprehension, for to appreciate something, one must first understand it. Appreciation is more affective, while comprehension is more cognitive. Have you ever heard someone tell a joke you did not think was particularly funny, but that you appreciated nevertheless? You might not like knock-knock jokes, but you can appreciate the riddle format, especially in a child's humor development. The reverse is also possible. One can cognitively comprehend a joke and yet not really appreciate it.

Appreciation requires comprehension of the material. Greater appreciation requires a moderate amount of cognitive challenge, while less appreciation results from humor that is either too easy or too difficult to comprehend. Children generally prefer humor that they can understand and derive considerable enjoyment from figuring out jokes. Often, optimal cognitive challenges enhance one's humor appreciation.

The appreciation of linguistic humor emerges and develops during the concrete operational stage (generally purported to be between the ages 7 through 12). Children at this stage of cognitive development often perceive more abstract relationships and appreciate the discrepancies between logical relationships and events. Although children can begin to appreciate humor before this stage, appreciation is rarely language-dependent. Comprehension is instead based on the incongruities that exist in nonlinguistic contexts (e.g., forms of visual or auditory humor such as a "pie-in-the-face" or a funny noise or sound often found in a cartoon episode). The ability to comprehend and use humor that comes from the manipulation of language (verbal humor) usually develops later.

The intellectual challenge presented by a joke or riddle is related to the individual's appreciation of it. However, the appreciation and production of humor depend to some degree on the level of the child's knowledge base; the development of logical, symbolic, and abstract reasoning abilities; and language development.

## Humor Mirth Response

Facial mirth response is defined as the spontaneous response to humorous stimuli. It can be measured on the following Likert scale, developed by Zigler, Levine, and Gould (1966): negative response—grimace (0), no response (1), half-smile (2), full smile (3), and laugh (4).

Zigler, Levine, and Gould (1967) also examined mirth response in relation to comprehension of humor. The degree of the mirth response depends upon the strength of cognitive congruence that existed between the cognitive demand features of the humor stimulus and the cognitive resources of the individual. When comprehending the joke taxes the individual's cognitive structure, the mirth response is maximal. Complete and easy comprehension does not result in the greatest amount of laughter. Often a child is unable to comprehend the joke correctly but sees it as funny for reasons (such as one particular feature of a cartoon) other than the correct one. When a child is questioned about a cartoon's funniness, he or she is confronted with the challenge of figuring out just why the cartoon is funny. Confronted with this challenge, the children do the very best they can. Through this trial and error process, children continue to develop their sense of humor.

# Humor Comprehension

The comprehension of humor is a developmental ability strongly related to both children's cognitive and language development. Comprehension of humor is the degree of cognitive congruence that exists between the cognitive demand features of the humor stimulus and the cognitive resources of the individual. Incongruity in humor results when there is either some variance between the body of the joke and the punch line or some violation of what is expected. So, to understand the ambiguity created in a joke, the child must have some knowledge of the concepts involved and some knowledge of any interrelationships between the words presented, as well as the ability to discriminate from possible alternatives. Language is often central to the comprehension of verbal humor, and humor can only occur when the child has a firm grasp of the concepts in question.

The comprehension of any particular joke may require a variety of cognitive processes. For example, the ability to condense material, the ability to become aware of and identify incongruities, and the ability to comprehend unusual verbal representations are important processes. We experience similar intrinsic pleasure when we attempt such mental activities as solving puzzles or brain teasers and decoding mysteries. Stated somewhat differently, the conceptual demands of a joke or a cartoon require a variety of cognitive functions.

# Humor Production

Humor production is the ability to create or produce humor. The humor produced is original. Increased humor production, comprehension, and mirth response are often associated with academics and social competence. Students who express these humor abilities are often viewed by teachers as more attentive, responsive, cooperative, and productive. Many times their peers view them as more popular, gregarious, happy, and as leaders. As you might expect, intellectual ability is moderately related to humor because the elements mirth response, comprehension, and production are significantly related to intelligence.

# Summary

The five elements of humor have been briefly introduced in this chapter. They are elaborated on and examples of each are provided in the chapters that follow. Even though they are separated into distinct chapters for the purpose of study, remember they are not only very interrelated, but often occur nearly simultaneously in the humor process.

# Humor
# Identification

**Activity:** Begin collecting and categorizing examples of oxymorons, puns, satire, idioms, tall tales, jokes, riddles, tongue-twisters, limericks, parodies, and ironies for your specific academic content areas. A labeled file folder for each subject is beneficial. These can then be used in a variety of related activities mentioned throughout this book.

This chapter begins with a brief discussion of the origins of humor. Next discussed are several popular theories that explain the nature of humor in human beings. Four forms of humor are then presented, followed by numerous categories of humor. Although some people say that nothing is less funny than a joke once it has been explained, an explanation is initially valuable for the purpose of studying humor. A classroom activity follows, including expected outcomes, classroom implications, benefits, and caveats. The chapter concludes with additional classroom activities.

## How Do We Identify Humor?

The element of identification in humor refers to the ability to distinguish and recognize something as humor, or to categorize an event or form of communication as humorous. Once we realize that humor is present, we can choose to analyze and categorize it. *Webster's Dictionary* defines *humor* as "quality of imagination quick to perceive the ludicrous or to express itself in an amusing way; fun; caprice; disposition; mood; state of mind."

## Origins of Humor

Why do we have a sense of humor? Where does our sense of humor come from? Have you ever wondered about the nature of humor? The word *humor* comes from the Latin *umor*, meaning "liquid," "fluid," or "moisture." In ancient Greece, a person's temperament was thought to be controlled by four humors (fluids). When in proper balance, a person was said to be "in good humor."

Too much of one of the fluids supposedly caused an imbalance in one's personality. Irritability occurred if yellow bile was disproportionate. One was said to be gloomy or melancholy if there was too much black bile present. Sluggishness prevailed for one with a predominance of green bile, and an oversupply of blood resulted in a person being confident or cheerful. Ironically, the prescription at the time for controlling this bad temperament, caused by excessive "humors," was laughter!

Only recently has the term "humorist" been used to describe someone who shows humor in their writing or speaking. We describe a person who possesses these skills in the literary or artistic use of humor as being funny. The term has taken on a more social connotation in recent years. In fact, the terms "comedian" or "comedienne" have become synonymous with the term "humorist."

# Theories of Humor

There are several major theories in the literature related to the numerous concepts and ideas about humor. Most were developed by famous philosophers as they studied human nature and the human condition.

## Incongruity Theory

Consider an example of humor caused by incongruity that may serve to better explain this theory. First, a "non-joke":

Boy: Daddy, Mommy was backing the car out of the garage and ran over my bike.

Daddy: Serves you right. How many times have I told you not to leave your bike in the driveway?

This entire situation is logical and possible; therefore we do not see it as funny in any way. However, if we substitute just two words, we transform this into a joke via a violation of expectancies, thus creating incongruity:

Boy: Daddy, Mommy was backing the car out of the garage and ran over my bike.

Daddy: Serves you right. How many times have I told you not to leave your bike *on* the *porch*?

Now it becomes a joke. When we visualize the car running over the bike *on the porch*, the situation becomes a humorous one. We did not hear what we expected to hear, and the incongruity created caused us to identify the humor in this situation.

Incongruity can take the form of contradiction, understatement, exaggeration, surprise, reversal, ludicrous, or the totally unreal. This generally causes cognitive dissonance—a sudden alteration. A sudden change in someone's point of view is almost always an essential ingredient for successful humor.

According to this incongruity theory, the source of humor in riddles and jokes (the most common examples of humor) may involve any or all of the following: understanding multiple meanings of words, metaphors, and idioms; detecting ambiguities and perceiving incongruity; and appreciating that the unexpected or a sudden shift of perspective is possible. Our ability to understand and use humor that is a result of manipulating language is a skill we begin to develop in childhood.

German philosophers Immanuel Kant (in 1790) and Arthur Schopenhauer (in 1819) are credited for developing this theory. The basis of this theory is that humor is created when we expect one thing and are suddenly presented with another. Humor, then, is the result of these unexpected connections. This mental trickery provides some relief to us from the rigors of logic, reason, and thinking. This theory emphasizes the mental or intellectual components of humor.

Humor is the outcome of these unexpected verbal or visual connections (incongruity). The incongruity in humor results when there is: 1) a discrepancy between the punch line and the body of a joke, and 2) a violation of expectancies. These may involve a) two conflicting sets of rules, b) two different frames of reference, or c) the reversal of figure and ground. The humor exists because the listener perceives the incongruity and then attempts to resolve it.

In addition, emotions play a large part in the creation of humor. As humor occurs, our attention, anticipation, tension, as well as the element of surprise all play a role in the process.

## Superiority Theory

Mark Twain once stated, "Everything is funny as long as it's happening to someone else!" This statement serves as a great example and introduction to the superiority theory of humor.

You may have heard your students laughing at a fellow student who made mistakes in the classroom, someone who mispronounced a word, someone who misspelled a word, or someone who answered "2 + 2 = 5." It happens frequently in any classroom. In these situations, someone is being disparaged, ridiculed, humiliated, or degraded as a result of making a mistake. As long as no one seems to be getting hurt, we sometimes believe this is acceptable and humorous. It is, however, debatable how much hurt or pain the recipient of this humor is truly experiencing.

This behavior also occurs daily in society. We tend to stereotype individuals and groups by attributes and characteristics. We often tell jokes about other people (world leaders, "the boss," etc.), occupations (doctors, lawyers, teachers, politicians, etc.), institutions (the federal government, the judicial system, the IRS, etc.), races (Black, American Indian, Hispanic, etc.), religions (Catholics, Jews, etc.), and nationalities (Irish, Italian, Polish, etc.). The purpose is often to inflate our own egos or deflate those individuals or institutions that we feel are superior. Interestingly, humor in these instances may also be viewed as a somewhat less obvious form of prejudice. Our notion of acceptable and unacceptable humor often begins in childhood in two primary environments: the home and the school.

As human beings, we receive pleasure when we see ourselves as better off than others. We pick on those less fortunate by poking fun at them, resulting in a form of self-glorification. Plato, Aristotle, Cicero, Descartes, and Bacon all took the view that laughter occurs when some flaw, imperfection, or deficiency is seen in others as we compare them to ourselves. British philosophers Thomas Hobbes (in 1650) and Alexander Bain (in 1880) advocated this theory of humor emphasizing the emotional components of humor.

To sum up the superiority theory of humor, we often laugh at the expense of others. A good way to test this theory is to ask yourself, Would this be funny if it had happened in the same way to me? This may be a good lesson to teach to students. In a situation like this, the "joker" rarely identifies with the "jokee."

## Relief/Release Theory

A third major theory was advanced by Freud during the twentieth century. According to the relief/release theory, laughter gives us some temporary freedom from the numerous restrictions under which we live our daily lives. Challenged are the notions of:

- ◆ constraints of conventionality

- ◆ inhibitions of sexual and aggressive desire

- ◆ the rigidity of logic

- ◆ our own egos

The relief/release theory emphasizes the social and behavioral components of humor. In this case, humor may be used to rebel against repressive or uncontrollable (whether real or perceived) elements of society. We make jokes against the hallowed institution of the Internal Revenue Service because we are controlled by it and often feel powerless when dealing with it. Similar jokes are made about life, death, and humanity in general and, through this, perhaps we find common bonds and a common strength.

An example of using humor for relief/release is when someone at a meeting uses humor to add a little levity to a tense situation or discussion. This allows everyone to laugh for a moment, break away from the topic at hand for a minute or two, regroup their thoughts, and begin addressing the issue, perhaps with a new perspective.

## Additional Theories

A number of additional theories can be found in the literature. They are continuously being researched and developed. The following represent a short list:

◆ Humor is a form of play, a reversion to childish innocence (Eastman, 1936).

◆ Humor is an antidote to inflexibility, a natural way of reminding ourselves of the ridiculousness of rigidity (Bergson, 1911).

◆ Humor exposes the truth; it rips away our veils of pretense and exposes the truth of human nature and human affairs (White, 1953).

# Four Forms of Humor

Some of us are not witty or cannot remember funny stories or jokes. You can begin to add humor to your teaching repertoire and daily classroom activity via the collection of humor you began as described in the beginning of this chapter. You will notice a variety of humor forms in the examples you collect. I identify four main forms of humor: figural, verbal, visual, and auditory. As we begin to examine humor, any example of humor can be easily categorized into one of these forms.

## Figural

Figural humor includes the following: comic strips, cartoons (including animation), and caricatures. These forms of figural humor appear in a variety of media, including television, movies, books, newspapers, and magazines, and involve the use of drawings to deliver the humor.

Most kids love to read comic books. These usually tell stories using cartoon characters involved in an often humorous story or adventure. Many of us rarely miss reading the comic page or "funnies" carried in our daily or Sunday local newspapers. These are usually comprised of two forms of comics: multiple-panel comics telling a story in one strip (e.g., *Calvin & Hobbes, Blondie, Arlo & Janis*, etc.) or in serial (continuous) fashion (e.g., *Rex Morgan, MD; Dick Tracy; Spiderman*; etc.). Comics can also take the form of single-panel strips (e.g., *The Far Side, The Lockhorns, Ziggy*, etc.). Comics, a thoroughly American institution, recently celebrated a 100th birthday (R. C. Outcault's The "Yellow Kid" - 1895 was considered the first American comic strip).

Animated cartoons made their first appearance in the movies. Walt Disney created Oswald, the Lucky Rabbit, in 1927. Mickey Mouse made his film debut in *Steamboat Willie* in 1928. Feature-length animated films, commonplace today, were born with the premier of *Snow White*, four days before Christmas 1937.

Also, consider caricatures, which are most often found on the editorial page. Most editorial cartoonists (e.g., Herbert Block) use caricature (along with exaggeration and political satire) to create these forms of figural humor. ◄

## Verbal

Verbal humor includes the following: jokes, puns, riddles, satire, anecdotes, comic simile, comic metaphor, hyperbole, irony, limericks, parody, tall tales, yarns, tongue twisters, and wit. These forms of verbal humor involve the use of language and often depend on the use of incongruity as demonstrated through contradiction, understatement, exaggeration, surprise, or reversal.

Denise: What's black and white and red (read) all over?
Steven: A newspaper.

Additional examples can be found in chapter 1. ◄

## Visual

Visual humor includes the following: sight gags, practical jokes, clowning, impersonations, impressions, pratfalls, and slapstick. This form of humor is dependent on visual cues for the humor to be effective.

## ➤ EXAMPLES

These forms of humor (sometimes referred to as sight gags) are often nearly hidden in the "background." For example, in one of the Three Stooges films, the three pretend to be bakers. When the cake is taken out of the oven, it "falls." They try to inflate it using natural gas. They forget about it, and as we see a conversation between them and a customer in the foreground, the cake is ever-expanding (inflating) in the background. We anticipate an explosion, thus the humor. Imagine "watching" the Keystone Cops, the Three Stooges, or any of the "Naked Gun" films if you could not see. You would probably be incredibly confused and not comprehend most of the intended (visual) humor. ◄

## Auditory

Auditory humor includes the following: impersonations, impressions, noises, and sounds. This form of humor is dependent on auditory cues for the humor to be effective.

## ➤ EXAMPLES

If you ever watched the television show "All in the Family," you probably remember laughing along with the audience every time Archie Bunker flushed that toilet. Now, you never saw that famous toilet, nor the Bunker bathroom, but you laughed at the timing of that flush in the story. Comedians also create sounds while performing that are designed to elicit a laugh. Impressionists such as Rich Little also use their voices to impersonate famous people. Victor Borge is an excellent example of a comedian who used auditory humor. One of his famous routines involved making noises when he spoke for each punctuation mark used in the sentence. He had a strange sound for a period, a different one for a comma, and so on. When he spoke, he inserted these sounds. ◄

## Categories of Humor

Just as any example of humor can fit into one of the four forms of humor, it can also be ascribed to a category. Mindess et al. (1982) divided humor into 10 basic categories. In their book *The Antioch Humor Test: Making Sense of Humor* (see "References"), the authors developed a test and provided an analysis for an individual's scores and themes. Briefly described below are the various categories.

## 1. Nonsense

Some humor may be categorized as silly, foolish, playful, or lighthearted. It may also border on the absurd. Knock-knock jokes fall into this category. For example:

> Knock, knock.
> Who's there?
> Banana.
> Banana who?
> Knock, knock.
> Who's there?
> Banana.
> Banana who?
> Knock, knock.
> Who's there?
> Orange.
> Orange who?
> Orange you glad I didn't say banana?

In contrast, perhaps the most sophisticated and complex form of nonsense humor ever created is the classic Abbott and Costello's "Who's on First?" routine. This all-time great routine from radio's golden age represents the pinnacle of wordplay. The routine worked equally well in vaudeville and in the movies.

## 2. Philosophical

Philosophical humor examines daily events related to the human condition. We discover humor when we are able to detect and perhaps appreciate the hypocrisy of a situation. Topics of philosophical humor include belief systems, relationships, religions, and the ultimate—the meaning of life itself. The following joke is an example of this humor category:

> A group of scientists wanted to build the quintessential computer. Having constructed it, they asked it the question: "Is there a God?" The computer's lights blinked for several seconds, then produced a piece of paper with the answer: "Now there is!"

Anyone still somewhat skeptical about the computer age can relate to this joke and the intended humor.

## 3. Social Satire

Similar to philosophical humor, social satire is often sophisticated humor that makes a statement about the human social condition. Such satire pokes fun at the establishment, authority figures, social institutions, and conventional social practices. Examples include:

Military intelligence is an oxymoron.

Once Democrat politician William Jennings Bryan, finding no stage at a country meeting on which to stand, climbed up on a manure spreader and said to the crowd, "Ladies and Gentlemen! This is the first time I have addressed an audience from a Republican platform!"

## 4. Sexual

Sexual humor most often takes the form of jokes, riddles, limericks, and anecdotes. Humorists such as Thurber and filmmakers such as Woody Allen often provide humor dealing with appreciation and tension between the sexes. This form of humor may range from mild flirting (fun) to outright crude or lewd (obscene) subject matter.

## 5. Hostile

Hostile humor usually involves some form of direct put-down of someone. This humor may attack someone's dignity or insult them in some other way. Depending on your point of view, the following examples from *Classic Comebacks* (1981) may also be samples of clever wit, due to the immediacy of the comeback:

Lady Astor once told Winston Churchill, "If you were my husband, I would put poison in your coffee!" Churchill immediately responded, "If you were my wife, I would drink it."

A pushy Hollywood social climber tried to force herself upon Groucho Marx by saying that she was an old friend. Groucho looked at her for a moment and said, "You know, I never forget a face . . . but I think I'll make an exception in your case."

Will Rogers told the story of a stranger who approached him in Will's hometown and asked, "Do you have a criminal lawyer in town?" "A lot of us think so," Will drawled, "but no one's been able to prove it yet."

## 6. Demeaning to Men

These are often referred to as "dumb men" jokes, and are designed to put down or otherwise discredit men. Not surprisingly, they are more enjoyed by women and most often told by women.

Q: How can you best get your man to exercise?
A: Put the remote control between his toes.

Q: What's the difference between government bonds and men?
A: Government bonds mature!

Q: Why is it easier to psychoanalyze a man than a woman?
A: Because, when he needs to revert to a childlike state, a man is nearly there.

## 7. Demeaning to Women

These are often designed to put down or otherwise discredit women. Not surprisingly, they are more enjoyed by men and most often told by men. Good examples of this form of humor include the "dumb blonde" jokes. For example:

Q: How do you know the blonde secretary has been at your word processor?
A: There's white-out on the screen.

Q: Why did God make a man before a woman?
A: He didn't want advice about how to do it.

## 8. Ethnic

Ethnic jokes put down or ridicule a particular group of people. Jokes are often aimed at Blacks, Hispanics, Poles, Russians, Italians, Irish, Iranians, as well as Catholics, Jews, Moslems, Baptists, and so on. Some individuals may find these jokes humorous; others find them offensive. Some appreciate the humor, while others equate it to a racial or religious slur. Interestingly, it is often acceptable for a Black to tell other Blacks a joke about Blacks. The same is true for any other group. It is amazing how often people repeat these jokes, never realizing that they are participating in a form of bigotry, racism, and prejudice.

Examples include:

"How many Polacks does it take to . . .?"

"There was a Jew, a Catholic, and a Baptist . . ."

"A Polack, an Irishman, and an Iranian were . . ."

However, some people use these jokes purposefully to denigrate, demean, or put down others. They often disguise their intent, claiming, "I was only joking," "It was only a joke," or "What's the matter? Can't you take a joke?"

## 9. Sick

Sick humor often pokes fun at deformity, death, and disease. Common jokes over the years have included "moron" jokes, Helen Keller jokes, and "dead baby" jokes. Recently, a number of stand-up comedians (Chris Fonseca, Geri Jewell, etc.) have built an entire comedy routine around their disability.

## 10. Scatological

This form of "bathroom" humor includes bodily noises and bodily functions. Many consider this form of humor to be too raunchy to be used in public.

Although examples of humor generally fall into only one of the four forms of humor, as detailed earlier, these examples often may be able to be placed into more than one category. For example, a joke such as:

It's the year 2095. Scientists have discovered people can become smarter by eating the brains of recently deceased smart people. The brains are now sold in the grocery store. A young man seemed puzzled over the prices for the following:

—Assistant professors' brains    $ 5.00 per pound

—Associate professors' brains    $10.00 per pound

—Full professors' brains    $25.00 per pound

—Deans' brains    $200.00 per pound

The young man said, "I can see why it doesn't cost much for the Professors' brains, but why does it cost so much for the Deans' brains?"

The grocer replied, "Son, do you know how many Deans it takes to get a pound of brains?"

The previous joke is cross-categorical, as it can be considered social satire, philosophical, hostile, sick, and demeaning to a group of people. The joke combines five of the ten categories previously discussed. Many forms of humor, when analyzed, are cross-categorical.

Certainly, the number of categories of jokes cannot be limited to a mere 10. Consider these additional categories offered by Mosak (1987)

## Double Meaning

The double meaning includes puns and double entendres. For example:

Chris: What has 18 legs and catches flies?
Beth: A baseball team.

The humor is accomplished in the previous lexical joke due to the multiple meaning of the word *flies*.

In the following pun, the humor is created by the play on words:

Eric: Why does it take a runner longer to run from second to third base than from first to second base?
Brian: Because there's a shortstop in between!

## The Surprise

The surprise is effective because it sneaks up on you. It comes out of nowhere. It catches you off-guard. You would never have guessed it or thought of it. You were not expecting it! For example:

Missy: What animal can jump higher than a house?
Mary Alice: I don't know. What?
Missy: Any animal. Houses can't jump!

## The Reversal

Riddles commonly are dependent on a reversal of unusual expectations. For example:

Doris: What did one flea say to the other as they went strolling?
Bill: Shall we walk or take the dog?

## The Contradiction

Sometimes referred to as logic that is illogical, this form of humor is effective because it presents the listener with internal contradictions. Notice the contradictions in each of the following examples:

Groucho Marx was once asked to join a posh country club. His response, "I wouldn't belong to any club that would have me as a member."

"Politics is too serious a matter to be left to the politicians."
—Charles de Gaulle

Middle age is that time when people would do anything to cure their latest ailment—except giving up what's causing it.

## The Ludicrous Story

These stories are ridiculous or exaggerated. For example:

Alice: Doctor, you have to help me. For the last three years my brother has thought he's a chicken.
Doctor: Well, why didn't you come to me sooner?
Alice: We needed the eggs.

Mosak (1987) proceeds to describe several other categories of jokes, including:

◆ the "Nothing Sacred joke," which includes forms of irreverence, lampooning, and satire.

◆ the "In-Joke," which only the "in" group will comprehend.

◆ Black humor, in which we laugh at tragedy, believing the laughter makes us more human.

◆ sick humor, which is only thought to be funny by those considered emotionally disturbed, sadistic, or both.

◆ gallows humor, which grows out of tragedy when the oppressed group or individual tries to alter their situation by making fun of those who are persecuting them. This often serves as a confident rallying cry for all those in a similar situation. Groups like prisoners of war, freedom fighters, and convicted felons often use humor to enhance cohesion in the face of oppression or authority.

◆ self-disparaging humor, which draws attention, both favorable and unfavorable, to the user. This is a form of self put-down. It is also reasonably safe to use this humor in moderation, as you are not seen as "attacking" or making fun of others, rather yourself.

◆ topical humor, which is funny only at certain periods of time. If told after many years have passed, some would not comprehend the joke because of the historical reference, and others would not find it funny, as it would seem "out of place" (and time). Political and some social humor falls into this category.

We Americans often use humor of a topical nature to deal with disasters in this country and around the world. Soon after a disaster or incident involving a famous personality, we hear jokes and riddles within weeks. You may remember jokes about the following catastrophes or individuals:

◆ the *Challenger* explosion

◆ the Gulf War

◆ the famine in Ethiopia

◆ the raid in Waco, Texas

◆ Lorenna and John Bobbit

◆ Michael Jackson

◆ the O. J. Simpson trial

◆ Watergate

◆ Senator Gary Hart and Donna Rice

Telling some of these jokes today would not necessarily elicit laughter. Rather, they may only serve to confuse. The events made humorous may have happened years ago; thus the humor loses its effect. When dated political cartoons appear in history books, students rarely comprehend the humor without a great deal of explanation from the teacher. Imagine how difficult it might be to tell a joke about the Revolutionary War or the stock market crash of 1929 to people today.

# Classroom Activity—
# Illustrating a History Research Paper

In this chapter, we have discussed the importance of humor identification and the role it plays in the overall nature of humor. To gain further insight into the element of identification, try the following activity. It is designed for use with secondary students in a history class, but you can modify it for any age or any academic subject.

**Outcome:** To illustrate a history research paper with at least three political cartoons.

**Activity:** Have students select (or draw their own) three political cartoons related to their history research paper. One of the cartoons can be related to the main historical figure in the paper, and the other two should represent both sides (pro and con) of the political issue. Students should begin to collect political cartoons from local newspapers and national magazines, discuss them, and eventually share them for this project. For example, when writing a paper on the topic of the immigration, cartoons can relate to a variety of related issues: migrant workers, poverty, education, health issues, green cards, illegal aliens, and so on.

Ask students to explain their choice of cartoons, explain the relevance and connection to the subject, and then have them identify the humor by form and category.

**Classroom Implications:** When adding this additional requirement (explanation) to the paper, students must use creative thinking and higher-level thinking skills. Relating the humorous cartoon to the topic is an exercise in application, analysis, synthesis, and evaluation. You challenge the students' creativity as they search for connections between the cartoon and the topic. The resulting product is an example of mixed media—visual and the printed word.

## Additional Activities Related to Humor Identification

Here are more classroom-tested activities that may assist your students in experiencing and learning about the element of humor identification.

1. Create a bulletin board or learning center with examples of jokes, riddles, puns, satire, limericks, and so on. Label each humorous item. Students may also want to label the form and the appropriate categories of humor.

2. Share with students personally humorous anecdotes. Allow students the opportunity to volunteer their humorous experiences. Topics might include: "My most embarrassing moment," "My favorite comedy film," "My favorite comedy TV show," and so on. Students might also cartoon these events. Sharing these moments will often create a bond through the recognition of human vulnerability and will often demonstrate how we can take ourselves a bit less seriously. This also provides an opportunity for the teacher to discuss how we should laugh *with,* not *at,* those who make mistakes in the classroom.

3. Create a bulletin board where students can write words (or tape colored index cards with words) that they find particularly funny, such as "jujube," "zoot suit," "belch," and so on. A discussion of censorship may ensue.

4. Have students collect words related to humor. Students can use a thesaurus and then create a booklet of the words. These can be used in a general discussion of the forms and categories of humor.

5. Make a banner or mural (to be displayed in the classroom) with cartoons from various sources or student drawings. The display can portray a theme or current event.

6. Keep a bulletin board entitled "Potpourri of Humor." This can be changed every month. Students can display (with prior teacher preview and approval) sketches, graffiti, one-liners, caricatures, puns, jokes, oxymorons, signs, and quotes.

7. Write a math slogan using puns. For example: "Don't be square. Try geometry!"

## Summary

Humor has been observed and studied for hundreds of years, often by philosophers and those in the fields of sociology and psychology. Numerous theories have been developed to try to help us understand the nature of humor. I believe that the acknowledgment and recognition of the element of humor identification is made easier by remembering the categories of humor developed by Mindess et al. (1982) and Mosak (1987) and elaborated in this chapter. The next time you hear a riddle, joke, or pun, see if you can easily place it in one of the many categories of humor discussed in this chapter. Try the activities in this chapter with your students and see if they are better able to identify humor as they experience it in your classroom.

# 3   Humor Appreciation, or "I Can Appreciate the Humor, But I Don't Enjoy It"

**Activity: "Rate-a-Cartoon"** Begin each day or class period by placing a cartoon on the overhead projector. This works best if the cartoon is related to timely subject matter. Ask students to individually rate the cartoon on a 1–10 scale as to how "funny" they think the cartoon is. Allow them time to share their ratings with their peers. Peers can also help explain the cartoon if someone does not "get it." This enhances the comprehension of the cartoon's humor for all involved. Students must employ the higher-level thinking skill of evaluation as they rate the "funniness" of a cartoon. The activity also demonstrates how we all appreciate different types of humor to different degrees.

## How and Why We Appreciate Humor

A number of joke and humor categories were presented in the previous chapter. As you examined and studied the different categories of humor, you perhaps found yourself appreciating some categories more than others. Appreciation occurs in degrees; hence, you might have a stronger preference for some humor types than for others, and you might appreciate humorous items within a certain category more than others for a variety of reasons.

If I ask you to rate a cartoon, or if I give you five samples of humor and ask you to rate each of them on a 1–10 scale, you might rate each sample differently. This indicates that you prefer or appreciate each differently. If you ask different friends to rate the same samples of humor, the odds are very good that none of your ratings would match theirs. This demonstrates how individualized and personal the appreciation of humor truly is.

A range of emotions can accompany these types of humor and may affect your appreciation of them. For example, some people are embarrassed by the sexual or scatological humor categories. Some are outraged

**25**

by the sick, hostile, or demeaning humor categories. These emotions will have an effect on the types of humor you use and appreciate.

As discussed in chapter 1, humor appreciation is the second element related to humor. Appreciation of humor is an *affective* quality. We often hear jokes that we do not think are very funny, yet we appreciate the humor (to some degree) just the same. *Webster's Dictionary* defines *appreciate* as "to value justly."

Although many types of humor require the presence of some form and degree of incongruity, the presence of incongruity alone does not make something humorous. Humorous stimulus must be perceived and appreciated as potentially humorous to generate the desired effect.

In addition, humor appreciation is often the result of some degree of problem solving on the part of the recipient. Prerequisites include the expectation of humorous stimuli, the explanation of the humor, and the resolution that it is indeed humor. Finally, the appreciation can occur prior to, during, or after the resulting laughter.

It is difficult to differentiate humor appreciation from humor identification, comprehension, and mirth response. They are interrelated. Roget's *Thesaurus* lists *comprehend* and *understand* as synonyms for *appreciation*. In the process of experiencing humor, one must first identify something as humorous, then comprehend it. The resultant comprehension evokes a degree of mirth response based on enjoyment level of the humor. Once these three events have taken place, humor is truly appreciated. In other words, you cannot appreciate the humor if you do not first identify it, comprehend it, and respond to it!

## Humor Appreciation and Thinking

Some degree of thinking and problem solving is involved in humor. The appreciation of humor does require comprehension of the material. Appreciation of humor should be highest when the material requires some degree of challenge or effort. Appreciation is often low when the joke material is either too simplistic or too difficult to understand.

Humor appreciation involves not only cognitive processes (such as those needed for incongruity resolution), but also affective and emotional processes as well. Humor is a combination of an individual's objective point of view as well as any environmental factors evident, such as the presence of other people. Two distinct and interacting modes of thinking are occurring when humor is evident. One level is cognitive processing, involving the ability to achieve and recognize the incongruity, resolution, and other attributes that are present. The other level is emotional processing, a subjective mode, based on prior experience, environment, and some personal appraisal of joke quality. Expressive reactions to humor are not independent of social or external factors. For example, if other people are laughing, you are also likely to do so, whether or not you find the humor amusing.

These ideas begin to provide us with an insight into the interrelatedness of humor comprehension and humor appreciation. This explanation of the dual process may provide a way to understand how the setting or the context of the humor (for example, canned laughter or the presence of others) might influence the appreciation of humor. As described earlier, this may be independent of the structural properties of the humor (e.g., resolution, incongruity). This may explain why some audiences seem to laugh easily at anything, and why canned laughter or a laugh track is often used in television shows, even though we may often wonder, What's so funny? or That's not really that funny.

Language, a component of cognitive development, is crucial to most forms of humor. However, humor can also be appreciated at different stages, independent of language development. The appreciation of verbal humor appears and then continues to develop during the concrete operational stage of development (ages 7–12). Some children at this stage of cognitive development have the advanced ability to perceive more abstract relationships and therefore can appreciate more abstract forms of verbal humor. Although children can appreciate some forms of humor before this stage, the appreciation is often not dependent on any language ability. Appreciation, then, is based on the incongruities present in nonverbal situations (e.g., a crazy picture, "pie-in-the-face" type antics, and other forms of physical humor often found in cartoons).

On a related note, some students prefer the use of humorous items on tests, believing it reduces their test anxiety to some degree, although not necessarily improving their test performance. This is in keeping with the fact students do prefer a teacher who has and employs a sense of humor in the classroom. Johnson (1976) asked 1,800 students (ages 5–18) what attributes made a teacher "good." One of the teacher traits topping the list was having a sense of humor and a pleasant nature. Other researchers have surveyed students and obtained similar results. "Sense of humor" was a top item in the personal and social categories. It is clear that most of us delight in an environment in which humor is appreciated and encouraged. The school classroom is one such environment.

Students prefer and appreciate humor they can understand (appropriate to their level and language ability). Students also derive considerable enjoyment and a sense of accomplishment from figuring out jokes. It appears more intellectually challenging material (or at least material equal to the student's level) can enhance humor appreciation.

To summarize, it appears there is an interconnectedness of the cognitive and affective qualities of humor. Both the appreciation and creation of humor depend on an appropriate level of factual knowledge, the development of symbolic, logical, and abstract reasoning abilities, and the language development of each student.

## Humor Appreciation and Response

It is also important to distinguish between amusement and enjoyment when discussing humor appreciation. We must remember to laugh *with*, not at someone. However, it is possible to laugh at the actions or events that occur on a daily basis that generate a humorous response in us. For example, we can laugh when the man slips and falls on the banana peel. We may be amused at any number of things, including his actual act of falling, the physical position he is currently in, the expression on his face, or something he says. However, we are not necessarily enjoying his predicament. We are indeed amused at the situation.

Along the same lines, we can appreciate humor but not necessarily enjoy it. For example, let's say you are at a party and someone tells a joke that is demeaning to men, demeaning to women, or "puts down" a particular group of people (Catholics, Iranians, individuals with disabilities, etc.). You can appreciate the joke as intended to be humorous, however perhaps you don't laugh, or you might even leave in disapproval. You appreciated the joke as a form of humor, yet you did not enjoy it. Humor is very personal and individual, and we all prefer certain jokes and forms of humor to others.

## Humor Appreciation and Cultural Differences

Appreciation of humor is also related to culture, ethnicity, and group affiliation. When one identifies with a particular group or culture, special "in-group" humor occurs, often in the form of sayings, terms, slang, stories, pet names and nicknames, and situational joking. This humor is used to increase group camaraderie and create a special bonding. Members of the group are free to employ this humor and to direct it to themselves, others in the group, and toward "outsiders." Individuals not members of the in-group are often chastised for using any of the group humor. For example, a Black comedian can use certain derogatory terms for Blacks, but a white comedian may be considered a racist or bigot for using the same term or telling the same joke. This is related to the concept of "always obtain permission" prior to using the humor (as discussed more thoroughly in chapter 9).

The following are just a few of the categories "in-groups" can be based on:

♦ Gender (male, female)

♦ Nationality (Irish, Mexican, etc.)

◆ Race (Black, WASP, Hispanic, etc.)

◆ Political Affiliation (Democrat, Republican, etc.)

◆ Age (teenagers, senior citizens, etc.)

◆ Religious Affiliation (Jewish, Catholic, etc.)

◆ Disability (blind, deaf, cerebral palsy, etc.)

◆ Social Organizations (Lions, Moose, DAR, etc.)

◆ School Organizations (football team, debate club, etc.)

Shared knowledge, rituals, customs, beliefs, and behaviors specific to a group, along with a history of shared experiences and events, provide the catalyst for numerous forms of humor that are only comprehended and appreciated fully by members of the group. A new member or initiate of the group, or an outsider visiting, will often not comprehend the "inside jokes" made by members of the "in-group."

## Classroom Activity—Television One-Liners

In this chapter, we have discussed the importance of humor appreciation and the role it plays in the overall nature of humor. To gain further insight into the element of appreciation, try the following activity. It is designed for use with upper elementary or secondary students in any subject matter class.

**Objectives:** Encourage students to become active listeners and consumers of TV; to further develop students' appreciation of humor.

**Activity:** Design a bulletin board or window display with the titles of television situation comedies (sitcoms). Create a collage of pictures of the sitcom stars. Then begin to add one-liners from the shows. Encourage students to add one-liners from the shows and then add new titles, stars, and one-liners from their favorite sitcoms. A nice spin-off would be to ask the students to watch old sitcoms from the 60s and 70s (Nickelodeon's Nick-at-Nite, TBS, and other channels often air these old comedies). Compare and contrast the types of humor found in the "old" and the "new" television comedies.

**Classroom Implications:** This activity allows students an opportunity to increase their use of higher level thinking skills (by comparing and contrasting information) and creative thinking (by becoming active listeners and searching for the connection between the humorous "one-liner" and the character). Besides, asking students to watch television comedies as "homework" may immediately endear you to the students.

# Additional Activities Related to Humor Appreciation

1. Display humorous literature and information about authors whom students are interested in. This can be a bulletin board display, learning center, or library table. Examples could include Mark Twain, Judy Blume, and Beverly Cleary.

2. Use humorous sentences when giving spelling tests.

3. Read to students a humorous passage daily at a specific time. Start with works of Shel Silverstein, William Coles, and Jack Prelutsky. Check with librarians for additional suggestions.

4. Tell the class each day that you will make at least one "intentional mistake." This can be verbal or in writing. Perhaps all who catch the teacher "being wrong" can earn one extra credit point for the day.

5. Sing a humorous song each day.

6. Keep a notebook (journal) and make a conscious effort each day to watch (stop, look, and listen) for work-related humorous events. Just as in the previous suggestion, you will begin to build a file of material for future use.

7. Set up a bulletin board in the faculty lounge. This way you can share humorous material with fellow teachers that might not be appropriate for students. Encourage coworkers to contribute signs, anecdotes, jokes, sayings, work-related cartoons, caricatures, and other developmentally appropriate, yet tasteful humorous items.

8. Read books by various humorists. Anthologies relevant for junior and senior high school students include the works of Will Rogers, Mark Twain, Ben Franklin, Ogden Nash, O. Henry, and E. B. White. The librarian can be of assistance in this endeavor.

9. Develop your "comic vision" by watching and looking for "signs" of humor around you. Watch television commercials and read billboard advertising and newspaper headlines for an especially rich source of material. Several now well-known signs include:

   ◆ Sign on a music store door—"Bach in a minuet. Gone Chopin."

   ◆ Sign in a diet clinic—"A word to the wide is sufficient."

   ◆ Frozen food counter ad—"The best meals you ever thaw."

*Reader's Digest* is a good source for material. A book of newspaper headlines entitled *More News of the Weird* by Shepherd, Kohut, and Sweet, provides actual newspaper clippings of real news stories. Examples of this form of humor include:

◆ Annette Montoya, 11, of Belen, NM, and her parents were arrested for forgery after Annette, in the company of her father, attempted to open a bank savings account with a $900,000 check. She said she earned the money doing "some yard work."

◆ Harold Womack, 51, of Phoenix, AZ, thought he could get his Porsche 924 out of a cinder pit at the Sunset Crater National Monument by using a 20-ton steamroller he spotted nearby. Womack drove the steamroller over to his car and hopped off to attach a chain. The steamroller kept rolling and flattened the car.

◆ Police in Van Nuys, CA, arrested Dennis Alston on charges of forging checks, then released him when he posted bail with a $1,500 cashier's check. It turned out to be a forgery!

10. Begin collecting excuses students bring. These may include notes regarding lack of permission, absences, and tardiness. Richard Lederer, in his book titled *Anguished English: An Anthology of Accidental Assaults Upon Our Language*, devotes an entire chapter to this topic. Begin writing creative excuses students give in class for not doing homework, not completing assignments, performing poorly on a test, why someone was fighting, etc. These could also lead to an interesting, more serious discussion, of responsibility, commitment, and dependability. Some examples of student excuses include:

◆ "Dear School: Please eckuse John being absent on Jan. 28, 29, 30, 31, 32, and also 33."

◆ "Please excuse Ray Friday from school. He has very loose vowels."

◆ "Please excuse Gloria from Jim today. She is administrating."

◆ "Please excuse Harriet for missing school yesterday. We forgot to get the Sunday paper off the porch, and when we found it Monday, we thought it was Sunday."

11. Introductions. This activity works well during the first week of school. Everyone has a worksheet with 20 items. Allow 15–20 minutes. Students are forced to really "mix" and begin to get to know each other. Each student must find someone in the class that has had one of the 20 items happen to them.

They may sign their name or initial beside the number. Examples include a student who:

◆ Has been to another country.

◆ Likes spinach.

◆ Thinks Ed McMahon or Conan O'Brian is a good comedian.

◆ Has had an embarrassing moment in front of more than 20 people.

12. Present a variety of cartoons from newspapers and magazines to the students. Have students rate each cartoon for "funniness" on a 1–5 scale, with 1 being "not at all funny" (some kids might say "dumb" or "lame") and a 5 being hilarious (allow students to create their own scale and descriptors). Students can then discuss the fact that different cartoons are funnier than others to different people for a variety of reasons (humor appreciation).

## Summary

It is important for teachers to understand the role humor appreciation plays in the classroom. Students' appreciation of humor has a role in the teaching and learning process. Humor in children has been traditionally viewed as either a sign of hostility and aggression or as some indicator of psychosocial development. Now, perhaps, it can be viewed as a useful guide to cognitive development.

Certain benefits may be achieved if the teacher appreciates the role appropriate humor can play in the classroom. Humor may relax tensions, provide conduits for otherwise unacceptable behavior, and allows a student to be more conducive to effective interchanges with others. There is also a relationship between creativity and humor. Such humor may help to maintain the variety, interest, and motivation so necessary for learning to occur in the classroom environment.

I offer the following thought in conclusion of this chapter concerning humor appreciation. Humor is not just jokes, or puns, or cartoons, or satire. It is not laughter or smiling. It is an attitude. How you choose to look at your work, your relationships with people, your life—is an attitude. Remember, take yourself lightly. Consider using humor to help achieve the balance! (You might want to skip now to the chapter on the benefits of humor.)

Remember as you think about humor appreciation that it is a very personal and individual attribute, varying in degree. There is nothing that is funny to everyone. At the same time, anything is potentially funny to somebody.

# 4

# Mirth Response, or "A Serious Look at Laughter"

**Activity:** Collect and display quotations about humor and laughter. Encourage students to add to the collection. Display these on a bulletin board or learning center. Ask the students to explain the quotations and perhaps tell something about the author. Libraries contain books of quotations like the following:

"Wrinkles merely indicate where smiles have been."
—Mark Twain

"Laughter is the shortest distance between two people."
—Victor Borge

"Better to remain silent and be thought a fool than to speak out and remove all doubt."
—Abraham Lincoln

"When humor goes, there goes civilization."
—Erma Bombeck

## What Is Mirth and Mirth Response?

What is mirth? *Webster's Dictionary* defines *mirth* as "gaiety; merriment; joyousness; laughter." Spontaneous mirth response, then, is the response to humorous stimuli.

Take a moment to read, think about, and enjoy the following quotations related to mirth and laughter:

"Mirth is God's medicine."
—Henry W. Beecher

"Humor . . . is essentially a complete mystery."
—E. B. White

"Among those whom I like, I can find no common denominator; but among those I love, I can: all of them make me laugh."
—W. H. Auden

"Laughter is, after speech, the chief thing that holds society together."
—Max Eastman

"He who laughs, lasts."
—Norwegian Proverb

"Men have been wise in very different modes; but they have always laughed in the same way."
—Samuel Johnson

"The jester is brother to the sage."
—Arthur Koestler

"If you wish to glimpse inside a human soul and get to know a man . . . just watch him laugh. If he laughs well, he's a good man."
—Dostoevsky

"Few would deny that the capacity for humor, like hope, is one of humanity's most potent antidotes for the woes of Pandora's Box."
—George Vaillant

The average four-year-old laughs 400 times a day. The average adult laughs 15 times a day! Why? Why does our use of humor and laughter diminish so in adulthood? Why do we begin to laugh only at certain times and only in certain places? Here are a few possibilities:

◆ "Stop being silly!"

◆ "Don't be ridiculous!"

◆ "Act your age!"

◆ "Act grown up!"

◆ "Be polite!"

◆ "Stop acting foolish!"

◆ "Follow the rules!"

◆ "Mind your manners!"

◆ "Don't rock the boat!"

◆ "What will your parents say?"

◆ "Wipe that silly smile off your face!"

Do any of these phrases sound familiar? Have you ever heard them before? Have you ever uttered any of them to the students in your classroom or to your own children?

Smiling and laughing are common behaviors in most people. We read the morning cartoons, laugh at each other's jokes at work or school, and watch situation comedies on television in the evening at home. Yet, another clear but conflicting message pervades our society; don't laugh in school, or in church, or even at the dinner table. We will often stop telling a joke right in the middle of it if a certain person (minister, teacher, or child) enters the room. We only tell certain jokes in certain circles, or in "mixed" company. To some people, being a "grownup" or an "adult" means acting sober, somber, earnest, and serious at all times!

Although the act of laughing or smiling would seem very obvious and visible to most people, scientists have been studying it for more than 100 years. In fact, in 1872, Charles Darwin, when describing laughter, wrote, "The sound of laughter is produced by a deep inspiration followed by short, interrupted, spasmodic contractions of the chest, and especially of the diaphragm . . . From the shaking of the body, the head nods to and fro. The lower jaw often quivers up and down, as is likewise the case with some species of baboons when they are much pleased . . . during laughter the mouth is opened more or less widely, with the corners drawn much backward, as well as a little upwards; and the upper lip is somewhat raised." Somehow, even his serious description of laughter seems somewhat humorous to me!

## Stages of Laughter

Although mirth is ambiguous at best as well as difficult to discriminate and categorize, Zigler, Levine, and Gould (1966) constructed the Children's Mirth Response Test and administered it to elementary aged children. Their overall findings indicated a general positive relation between cognitive level and the comprehension of the humor and a complex relation between comprehension and mirth response. Spontaneous facial mirth response was scored using the following five-point Likert scale:

| | | |
|---|---|---|
| 0 | = | negative response (grimace, etc.) |
| 1 | = | no response (blank stare, etc.) |
| 2 | = | slight or half smile |
| 3 | = | full smile |
| 4 | = | laugh |

I present this scale to demonstrate the degree of variance in mirth response. To the trained observer, as many as 8–10 smile differentiations could exist. I believe this is important, as it is generally believed people who smile more are more well-liked. I could easily take "laugh" and develop it further, perhaps into:

1 = snicker
2 = giggle
3 = chuckle
4 = belly laugh for 15+ seconds.

I conducted a study with elementary and secondary students and discovered those students identified as gifted scored significantly higher on mirth response to verbal humor than did students from the general population (Shade, 1991). Others have also studied mirth response in gifted students and discovered it to be significantly related to IQ. I believe this increase in mirth is partially due to communicative competence and partially due to comprehension.

I propose laughter is actually a four-stage process:

**Stage 1—Expectation:** When we expect or anticipate something is going to be humorous, we are in a "set-up" mode. We are awakened or aroused to the potential for laughter. For example, when we attend what has been advertised as "the comedy event of the year; a four-star, two-thumbs up comedy" we are in a mindset of anticipation. We expect to laugh and laugh a lot!

Stand-up comedians refer to this stage as the setup/punch format. The "setup" is the line or two leading up to the "punch." The "punch" is the "punch line" that elicits the laughter. The setup lures and entices the audience, while the punchline usually forces an emotional and physical reaction: laughter.

**Stage 2—Explanation:** After the expectation stage has occurred, the explanation process is initiated in an attempt to understand, explain, or make sense of the incongruity presented. One often refers to past experiences to attempt to accomplish this task.

**Stage 3—Resolution:** The incongruities are now resolved and the recipient determines the result to be humorous in nature. One's attitudes, beliefs, morals, and values come into play at this stage, which is why humor is such an individual and personal experience.

**Stage 4—Laughter:** When everything "makes sense," that is, it is comprehended and understood to be humorous, laughter results from the range of mixed emotions experienced throughout the four-stage process. Koestler described getting the punch line of a joke as "the intellect turning a somersault."

## Additional Thoughts on Mirth

I offer the following additional thoughts and observations on laughter:

1. Laughter is very potent. Laughter has the potential to:

   ◆ change a "minus" situation into a "plus."

   ◆ change fragmented feelings into connected ones.

   ◆ reverse the process of anxiety and depression.

   ◆ move us toward appropriate action.

2. Laughter can control pain. Laughter has the potential to distract attention, reduce tension, change expectations, and increase the production of endorphins in the brain. All these can be beneficial to both student and teacher in the classroom.

## Classroom Activity—Laugh at Yourself

In this chapter, we have discussed the importance of mirth response and the role it plays in the overall nature of humor. To gain further insight into the element of mirth response, try the following activity. It is designed for use with elementary or secondary students in any subject matter class.

**Outcomes:** To teach students it is okay to laugh at yourself and with others; possibly enhancing self-esteem; to not take yourself too seriously.

**Activity:** Sing a humorous song or tell a humorous story. Audio tape the session. Then replay the tape. See if the students can identify their classmates by their laugh. Discuss why individuals thought some things were funny. A spin-off activity is to teach the signs (signing) for humorous words. Use the signs with each other. Make a class chart of what types of things make people laugh.

**Classroom Implications:** This activity will help increase the students' higher level thinking skills and their creative thinking skills. They must listen carefully, discriminate between the laughs, then evaluate and make a selection. The behaviors of guessing and risk-taking are also encouraged and enhanced through this activity, which are behaviors necessary to creative thinking.

## Additional Activities Related to Mirth Response

1. Hold a "best joke" contest. Students can hold up cards in Olympic-style voting or use the old concept of an applause meter. Average the scores (math) and select the "Stand-Up Comedian of the Week."

2. Create a chart of "What makes people laugh?" Include words, events, people, movies, and television shows.

3. Smile more! This sounds incredibly simple. People who smile more are better liked. (Think about it, who would you rather be around?) The message: Take your work seriously and yourself lightly!

4. We all seem to have one or more students we refer to as a "class clown." Channel some of their excess energy to the study of the art of clowning. References might include books, old movies, and researching famous professional clowns to learn about makeup, tricks, props, and routines used in the profession.

## Summary

Why do people react differently upon hearing the same joke? The reasons are numerous, and include:

♦ not understanding it (comprehension).

♦ it may ridicule a particular individual or group.

♦ it may support the notion of superiority of an individual or group.

♦ it may attack or support an individual's core belief.

In summary, it can be said with confidence that we do smile and laugh in a variety of ways for a variety of reasons! I leave you with more intriguing quotations about mirth and laughter.

"Humor is a means of obtaining pleasure in spite of the distressing affects that interfere with it."
—Freud

"Humor at its best is a kind of heightened truth — a super-truth."
—E. B. White

"Laughter begins as a primitive shout of triumph."
—Stephen Leacock

"You don't stop laughing because you grow old, you grow old because you stop laughing."
—(Attributed to Michael Pritchard)

"The most wasted day of all is that on which we have not laughed."
—Sebastian Chamfort

"Every joke is a tiny act of rebellion."
—George Orwell

"Rigidity is the comic, and laughter is its corrective."
—Henri Bergson

"There are three things which are real: God, human folly, and laughter. The first two are beyond our comprehension. So we must do what we can with the third."
—John F. Kennedy

"Dictators fear laughter more than bombs!"
—Arthur Koestler

"Laughter and tears are meant to turn the wheels of the same machine of sensibility; one is wind power, and the other is water power. That is all."
—Oliver Wendell Holmes (1858)

# 5 Humor Comprehension, or "Oh, Now I Get It! Now That's Funny!"

**Activity: "Cartoon Caption Match"** Begin by collecting numerous and various single-panel cartoons from the newspaper or magazines. Remove the captions. On a worksheet or bulletin board, mix up the cartoons and a list of captions. Working individually or with a partner, students will attempt to match the correct caption with the appropriate cartoon. An interesting spin-off is to give half the students cartoons and the other half captions. Students must then wander the room and match up with their "partner." Reading, teamwork, and decision making skills will be simultaneously employed in this activity. The objective is for students to be able to correctly match captions with their single-panel counterparts.

## What Is Involved in Comprehending Humor?

This element of humor is the ability to cognitively understand humorous stimuli. *Webster's Dictionary* defines *comprehension* as, "the act of comprehending; the capacity of the mind to perceive and understand." More specifically, comprehension of humor can be defined as the degree of agreement or match that exists between the cognitive abilities of an individual and the specific cognitive demands of the humor presented.

What actually happens when we "get" the joke? Comprehension mediates the humor process and also contributes to the degree of personal gratification. We enjoy discovering or "getting" the point of a joke, and the more subtle and indirect it is, the greater the cognitive challenge and the greater the resulting pleasure.

# Prerequisites to Humor Comprehension

What are the prerequisites or requirements for one to comprehend humor? A variety of cognitive processes may be required to understand any particular joke. For example, condensing information, becoming aware of possible existing incongruities, and the ability to discriminate and comprehend unusual verbal representations are but a few.

Therefore, humor comprehension initially requires cognitive prerequisites at various levels and then the emotional experience of gratification. Both the cognitive (intellectual) and the affective (emotional) components are involved in the humor process. Part of the cognitive process is drawn from our experiences with conceptual patterns, behaviors, and ordinary expectations. For example, when I answer the door, I expect to see someone on the other side dressed in "conventional" attire. However, if I answer the door and the person is dressed in a gorilla suit with a diver's mask, snorkel, and a bunch of red balloons, I am presented with the incongruous. I have been led down one path and was forced to shift abruptly to another. Humor is often the result.

Scientists have for years believed all language and linguistic functions are the responsibility of the left hemisphere of the brain. The right hemisphere is now believed to be crucial to comprehending and relating parts of narratives and jokes to each other. As discussed previously, there are several parts to a joke (set-up, punch line, etc.) as well as the belief that emotion plus cognition play a part in humor. It appears humor requires an ambidextrous brain. Only when both hemispheres are working together can we appreciate the humor in a story or the punch line of a joke.

# Comprehension by Resolving Incongruity

Now, I will be the first to agree with the statement that nothing is "unfunnier" than analyzing or explaining a joke. However, at the risk of "ruining" several jokes, let's analyze the following and examine the criterial incongruities for each. What cognitive prerequisites (content area knowledge) to comprehension are necessary in the following forms of humor?

A man went to Cape Canaveral and asked the attendant if he could buy a ticket to the moon. "Sorry, sir," the attendant said, "the moon is full just now."

◆ The subject must identify the incongruity of the use of the concept "full" as an adjective or a noun (full as the opposite of empty in terms of capacity; a full moon).

> Brenda: How do you keep an elephant from charging?
> Rob: Take away his credit card.

◆ The subject must identify the incongruity that exists between the use of the word "charging" as it applies to each situation (elephant running and credit card use).

> Katie: If athletes have athlete's foot, what do astronauts have?
> Harry: Missile toe.

◆ The subject must identify the incongruity that exists between the meaning of the words "missile toe" *and* "mistletoe" and the fact that a missile is associated with astronauts.

> Dan: What did Mrs. Bullet say to Mr. Bullet?
> Betsy: We're going to have a B-B!

◆ The subject must identify the incongruity of the association between the words "B-B" and "Baby" *and* know that a BB refers to a pellet or projectile associated with a bullet.

> Missy: If there are five flies in the kitchen, how can you tell which one is a football player?
> Dorothy: It's the one in the sugar bowl.

◆ The subject must identify the incongruity of a play on words between a common "sugar bowl" on the kitchen table and the "Sugar Bowl" football game played each year during the New Year's Day holiday season.

In each of the examples above, the incongruity is resolved when we become aware of the humorous relationship between the punch line and the set up (the body) of the joke. In order to find any of the jokes amusing, the student must 1) comprehend a number of specific cognitive facts, 2) identify the incongruity presented, 3) resolve the incongruity based on a previous knowledge base, and 4) react to the joke (mirth response) to the degree the humor is appreciated.

Sometimes a child or an adult is unable to comprehend a joke correctly. They see it as funny for reasons other than the correct or logical one. Often they will focus on one particular feature of the cartoon and find it funny. The child realizes the situation is one in which a humorous response is expected, and confronted with this dilemma of trying to deduce just why the humor is funny, does the best he can. Laughter is occurring without true (or perhaps only partial) comprehension.

Younger children may appreciate and laugh at the following riddle. They laugh because others are laughing (social) even though they cannot offer the appropriate criterial incongruity, evidence comprehension is lacking:

Wade: How do you keep fish from smelling?
Tate: Cut off their noses.

One child might say, "It's funny because fish don't have noses," while another's reasoning might be, "A fish can't smell under the water."

Although it is important for teachers to be aware of the "humor levels" of their students related to each of the five elements of humor, it is difficult to easily or accurately assess these. Currently no formal assessments are available which are designed to directly assess children's comprehension and use of humor.

## Language and Humor Comprehension

What role does language play in humor, and especially in humor comprehension? For example, upon further examination, the comprehension of riddles involves each riddle presenting some form of misleading element that makes it difficult to guess correctly and a resolution factor that has the answer be somewhat sensible. These are combined to form the riddle. The understanding or comprehension is the link between the question and the answer.

The role of language development is at the core of humor development. The level of language mastery plays a primary role in the manner and degree to which humor can be either comprehended or expressed. Language development is a paramount prerequisite to humor comprehension, since most humor (verbal and figural) involves the use of words and language. For example, puns (verbal humor) employ the use of plays on words (substitutions of words; dual meanings—literal vs. figural; homonyms—to, too, two; etc.). How can one comprehend or appreciate this form of humor if one's language is not developed fully enough to understand the meanings of the words involved?

The receiver of the humor plays an important role in the joke-telling process. The passive role of the listener is an important element in a situation involving humor; a joke may lose its effect of laughter as soon as the listener is required to think too long or hard about it. The allusions made in a joke must be obvious and the omissions easy to fill, otherwise the joke loses its effect.

As stated previously, if jokes need to be explained, then they are often no longer funny. Jokes and other forms of humor are more effective if comprehended spontaneously. Some forms of humor require a moment of thinking, thus causing a "delayed reaction" of laughter. When we dissect a joke, it definitely neutralizes any humor. Also, when we spontaneously "get" a joke, we respond with laughter and are in a state of happiness, relaxation, and joy. When we don't "get" the joke, or need to have it explained to us, we are sometimes in a state of confusion or embarrassment, and must shift to an active, analytical state. This now becomes work instead of fun!

A wonderful example of humor at different cognitive levels simultaneously can be found in one of the most often read works of literature in American schools today, Lewis Carroll's *Alice's Adventures in Wonderland*. Many adults enjoy the following passage, while it is "over the heads" of some school children. Some may have trouble comprehending the intended humor in the following excerpt from Chapter Nine, a conversation between Alice and the Mock Turtle:

> "We had the best of educations - in fact, we went to school every day—"
>
> "*I've* been to a day-school, too," said Alice. "You needn't be so proud as all that."
>
> "With extras?" asked the Mock Turtle, a little anxiously.
>
> "Yes," said Alice: "we learned French and music."
>
> "And washing?" said the Mock Turtle.
>
> "Certainly not!" said Alice indignantly.
>
> "Ah! Then yours wasn't really a good school," said the Mock Turtle, in a tone of great relief. "Now, at *ours*, they had, at the end of the bill, 'French, music, and *washing*—extra.'"
>
> "You couldn't have wanted it much," said Alice; "living at the bottom of the sea."
>
> "I couldn't afford to learn it," said the Mock Turtle with a sigh. "I only took a regular course."
>
> "What was that?" inquired Alice.
>
> "Reeling and Writhing, of course, to begin with," the Mock Turtle replied; "and then the different branches of Arithmetic—Ambition, Distraction, Uglification, and Derision."

Now, some children (and maybe some adults) who read this will not comprehend the puns, satire, and sarcasm of Carroll. However, one of his cardinal rules in his writing was to never "write down" to children and to not be "sweet" or "cute."

Another example demonstrates the clever use of puns:

> "And how many hours a day did you do lessons?" said Alice, in a hurry to change the subject.
>
> "Ten hours the first day," said the Mock Turtle: "nine the next, and so on."
>
> "What a curious plan!" exclaimed Alice.
>
> "That's the reason they're called lessons," the Gryphon remarked: "because they lessen from day to day."

It is somewhat ironic many leaders in public school education today suggest or require reading this literary classic, and yet throughout it consistently provides a farcical treatment of public school education as well as satires on various theories of education! Unfortunately, some today find these parodies of education as applicable today as more than 100 years ago.

So, we all must be able to understand or comprehend the work in context to be able to fully appreciate the intended humor. Remember, to comprehend the humor, newly acquired concepts appear to become occasions for laughter only when the individual has acquired some degree of competency in their meaning and use. The alteration of words, sounds, or meanings may become a basis for humor only after conceptual thinking has developed.

## Studies in Humor Comprehension

Zigler et al. (1966) conducted a study to examine the relationship between cognitive development and humor appreciation in children. In this seminal work, they administered the Children's Mirth Response Test (CMRT) to a number of elementary-aged students. To assess comprehension, a scoring guide was developed employing the following categories:

0 = no comprehension
1 = partial comprehension
2 = full comprehension

Mean comprehension scores increased for all grade levels (grades 2–5) and were found to be statistically significant. These comprehension scores demonstrated a positive relationship to the students' mirth response scores in this study.

What is also proposed by this study is the notion that one's mirth response is partly a response to the joy of "getting the joke" as much as the content of the joke itself! This means we must be cognitively challenged (comprehending the humor), if we are to respond overtly with greater laughter (mirth response). Therefore, it follows, adults do not laugh at the same humor a child might laugh at with the same intensity due to the cognitive demand of the humor (see chapter 11).

I was also interested in the role that comprehension plays in humor. In a study conducted with elementary and secondary students, I discovered those students identified as gifted scored significantly higher on the comprehension of verbal humor than did students from the general population (Shade, 1991). Initially, I had developed a twenty-item instrument from 2,098 humorous items of verbal humor. These items were recorded onto an audio tape. Upon hearing the age-appropriate riddles, jokes, puns, and selections of satire, the students were asked for each item, "Why is this funny?" to assess their comprehension (in this case, the identification of incongruities). If students did not respond, they were asked, "Then, why would some people think it was funny?" Students were then rated on the three-point Likert scale of comprehension measure developed by Zigler et al. (1966). The students' responses were compared to a predetermined list of criterial congruities and criterial resolutions for each of the items on the final instrument. For example, after hearing the following joke, the student was asked why it was funny:

Tim: What geometric figure is like a lost parrot?
Sue: Polygon!

The student had to identify the incongruity that exists between the words. A polygon in geometry is a geometric figure. Polly is a common name for a parrot; hence the phrase "Polly gone" and the word *polygon*. Based on the response, the subject would receive 0 (no), 1 (partial), or 2 (full) points for comprehension. In summary, I discovered the gifted students performed statistically significantly higher in humor comprehension than the students in the general population, meaning they better understood the humor than did their counterparts.

Thus far, I have discussed various aspects of the element of comprehension and its role in humor. I now offer a different perspective. Yes, I have discussed the fact an individual must understand a joke to be able to identify it, appreciate it, and generate mirth response related to it. However, is it possible to measure the necessary prerequisite information an individual possesses required to comprehend the humor presented? For example, if I showed you a cartoon or told you a joke related to types of rocks or uses for a word processor, could you explain why the joke was funny, or why others might think it was funny? In your answer, I believe I could then measure your comprehension of academic material via your explanation of the cartoon or joke. We could then logically assume that you would need to know the material to explain the joke, and if you explained the joke, then you must know the material well enough to do so.

I conducted a study (Shade, in press) to examine the use of figural humor (cartoons) as an alternative assessment format for evaluating student comprehension. Participants were undergraduate special education majors. These students were administered a mid-term examination comprised of 12 cartoons selected for appropriateness of content to the particular university course. Hence, the students had to understand and know the academic content in order to respond to the related cartoons.

Comprehension of the academic content was measured by students' ability to identify at least one incongruity (Why is this cartoon funny?). The full points were awarded in the majority of cases for providing detailed explanations. Students also received points for correct answers to accompanying knowledge-based questions.

Analysis revealed the use of figural humor triggered possible nonconventional thinking in the students resulting in the generation of divergent answers not anticipated by the instructor. The atmosphere of acceptance created by the directions "Explain this cartoon. In other words, why is this cartoon funny or why do you think others might think it was funny?" allowed for various interpretations of the cartoons. Instead of the students trying to remember the *one correct answer*, students generated 13 different answer types for the first question, 17 different answer types for the second question, and so on.

It appears the use of humorous, relevant cartoons was effective in eliciting creative, divergent responses. The unexpected humorous stimuli triggered the generation of nonconventional thinking, producing more flexible (creative, yet relative) responses. There seems to be a consensus among educators that convergent thinking is heavily emphasized, almost exclusively, in our schools. The alternative assessment format demonstrated in this study has the potential to increase divergent thinking, an essential element of creativity. What then, makes or helps make creativity? Humor helps. Studies have found that the characteristic which sets highly creative students apart from high IQ students is a sense of humor. In rating personality characteristics, highly creative students placed a sense of humor near the top of their list.

In addition, humor increased the meaningfulness of the material and enhanced the learning and retention of such material by increasing associations between material to be learned and material students already knew. Some studies have demonstrated retention of material through the use of humorous examples is most effective when test items are based on relevancy of content taught. Therefore, always remember to keep the humor relevant to the academic content to avoid possible distractions.

It should be noted this study employed figural humor. For some students, other forms of humor may be more appropriate. For example, some students may be better able to comprehend jokes or riddles, while others work better with cartoons and comics. Teachers must remember to address individual differences and preferences when using appropriate humor to teach important concepts and content. In other words, the use of cartoons (figural humor) may be problematic for some students. Verbal humor (jokes, puns, riddles, satire, etc.) may be a better alternative for some.

## Additional Notes on Humor Comprehension

It takes at least two people to make a joke happen: the initiator(s) and the receiver(s). Some of the problems experienced by the receiver of the joke include:

- ◆ takes the joke the wrong way.

- ◆ does not comprehend or "get the joke."

- ◆ overreacts to the intended humor.

- ◆ does not realize it was meant as humor and now becomes upset.

- ◆ purposely declares, "I don't get it" to draw attention to oneself (becoming the center of attention by "playing dumb" or acting as the only one who doesn't get the joke).

- ◆ states, "I don't get it" due to being embarrassed by the humor (especially categories such as scatological, sexual, ethnic, etc.).

- ◆ does not want to "get" the humor because the subject matter is too close to the individual's "real life" situation; the person might then have to admit to some deficiency or problem.

There are also numerous reasons why we fail to comprehend a joke. Some include:

- ◆ unfamiliarity with the specific content. For example:

> There once was a spaceman named Wright,
> Whose speed was much faster than light.
> He set out one day,
> In a relative way,
> And returned on the previous night.

This limerick by an unknown author is an excellent example of content specific to space science. One would have to understand the various elements of Einstein's theories related to time and space travel to be able to fully comprehend and then appreciate this example of humor.

- ◆ humor is topical (not relevant; not timely). For example:

"Silent Cal" Coolidge was a man who knew when to keep his mouth shut. In fact, he rarely said much of anything. Early in his presidency a woman approached him at a banquet and said, "Mr. President, I made a bet with my husband that I could get you to say more than two words." Coolidge replied without hesitation, "You lose."

—(*Classic Comebacks* - 1981)

> Two Quaker women in a railroad coach were overheard
> in conversation about the forthcoming election. Says
> one, "I think Jefferson Davis will succeed."
> "Why does thee think so?"
> "Because Jefferson is a praying man."
> "And so is Abraham a praying man."
> "Yes - but the Lord will think Abraham is joking."
> —(Mindess et al., 1982)

Someone who did not know of these individuals or of events that surrounded and shaped these time periods might respond, "So, what's so funny?" or "I don't get it." Although the humor can still be comprehended and appreciated by some, it is somewhat timely. Any piece of humor related to a particular time period in history is apt to be troublesome to some as they attempt to comprehend the humor.

◆ failure to identify the incongruity present. For example:

> An old lady was sent on a seven-day ocean cruise paid for
> by her son. She wrote back to complain, "The food here on
> this ship is perfectly dreadful. And such small portions!"

One might not immediately discern the satire present in this story. If the food was indeed so bad, why would she want such large portions?

◆ failure to resolve the incongruity. For example:

> What has a bed, yet never sleeps,
> And has a mouth, yet never eats,
> And always keeps moving?
> Answer: A river

People might not get this, because they are not able to resolve the incongruities presented, especially in the first two lines, and then in all three lines combined.

It should be pointed out here that numerous professionals use humor for a variety of reasons (to make a point, to help an individual relax, to teach a concept, etc.). A caution: if the individual does not immediately comprehend the humor, or misinterprets the intended use, the application may "backfire."

# Classroom Activity—Cartoon Sequencing

In this chapter, we have discussed the importance of humor comprehension and the role it plays in the overall nature of humor. To gain further insight into the element of comprehension, try the following activity. It is designed for use with upper elementary or secondary students in any language arts related class.

**Outcomes:** To enhance a student's visual and verbal sequencing abilities.

**Activity:** Cut apart four-panel comic strips (such as *Charlie Brown* or *Garfield*) and place them in a letter-size envelope. Challenge students to arrange the segments in the correct sequence. Visual sequencing can be practiced by eliminating (using white-out) any words in the "conversation bubbles." Sequencing can be made more difficult by using eight-panel cartoons often found in the Sunday comics (*Blondie*, *Beetle Bailey*, *Hagar the Horrible*, and *The Born Loser*). Perhaps an even greater challenge is to then place several comic strip segments into the envelope. The student must first separate (discriminate) the segments by attribute, then sequence.

**Classroom Implications:** This activity is a good example of how there must be a cognitive match between the degree of agreement of the student's cognitive abilities and the specific cognitive demands of the humor presented. Visual sequencing must first be achieved, followed by the production of language-based humor. The skills of visual sequencing and the production of appropriate humor are both within the realm of higher level thinking and creative thinking.

# Additional Activities Related to Humor Comprehension

1. Study the humor of different areas of the United States (regional humor), other countries, or other cultures. Display a collection of jokes, cartoons, comic books, or humorous stories from these different locations. High schools often have foreign exchange students. These individuals could be interviewed on similarities and differences related to humor in literature, television, etc.

2. Learn the sign language for various humor words like smile, laugh, joke, riddle, etc.

3. Place a humorous item on each test you give. These can be bonus items at the end of the test (see section on using humor to assess comprehension).

4. Listen to humorous records, tapes, or CDs. Examples include "Weird Al" Yankovic, Bill Cosby, and Garrison Keillor. (Note: Remember to always preview this material.)

5. Listen or watch the classic Abbott & Costello's "Who's On First?" vaudeville comedy routine. The act is available on 16mm film, videotape, audio tape, and book formats. Have students practice the routine, focusing on timing, voice volume and pacing, enunciation, concentration, and delivery. Perhaps a "Who's On First?" contest would be motivating in April when baseball season begins and students' interests and minds are more concerned with after-school practices than on school.

## Summary

Several researchers have begun to study the element of comprehension and its relationship to humor (Shade, 1991; Zigler et al., 1966, 1967). It is also evident language is related to most forms of humor, especially verbal humor. Included here are additional thoughts about comprehension as it relates to humor:

◆ To understand humor, the listener must often disregard the literal interpretation of what is said and go beyond it to derive meaning from what is not literally stated. The understanding of words, metaphors, idioms, etc., is essential to the comprehension of most forms of humor, especially verbal humor. The ability to use and comprehend humor appropriately involves the manipulation of language. Metalinguistic skill and the corresponding cognitive skills are essential for one to comprehend humor.

◆ The comprehension of humor is developmental. It progresses from understanding the nonlinguistic humor common in early childhood to understanding humor based on language and language-related ambiguities during adolescence. As discussed earlier, this progression is related to the child's cognitive and language development.

In closing, I remind us of Winston Churchill's view on the comprehension of humor. As Churchill said, "It is my belief, you cannot deal with the most serious things in the world unless you understand the most amusing."

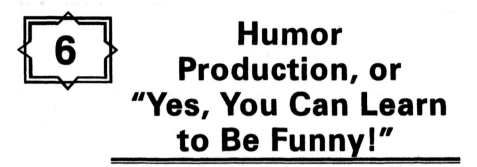

# Humor Production, or "Yes, You Can Learn to Be Funny!"

**Activity: "Fictionary"** The name of this activity is the result of combining "fiction" with "dictionary." Divide students into groups of five or six. Each group will need a dictionary, pencils, and sheets of paper. Select one student to be the "dictionary person." This person finds a word in the dictionary unfamiliar to all players. Everyone writes down the word on their paper. The "dictionary person" copies the correct definition, while other players make up a definition. All definitions are mixed up, then read aloud by the "dictionary person." Players then vote for the definition they believe is the correct one (the "dictionary person" does not play this round). The "dictionary person" then reads the correct definition. Players receive one point if they vote for the correct definition, and also receive one point for each vote cast for their personal "made up" definition. At the end of each round, a new player becomes the "dictionary person." This activity allows students to practice the creative thinking skills of fluency, flexibility, originality, and elaboration.

## Humor Production

This element of humor is the ability to create and deliver humorous stimuli. *Webster's Dictionary* defines the verb *produce* as, "to bring forth; to exhibit; to give birth to; to yield; to make; to cause." I like to use the synonym *create*.

## Benefits of Producing Humor

In the process of creating humor, a number of direct and indirect benefits may occur. These include:

- ◆ You may become wittier, funnier, and even more self-confident. The use of humor in any form of public speaking is often received very positively by the audience. This positive reception has the potential to boost one's self-confidence.

◆ You may gain (and possibly persuade others to gain) a new perspective on a situation through the appropriate use of humor.

◆ You may turn a negative, possibly painful situation into a more positive, pleasurable, funny experience.

◆ You may improve your risk-taking ability by producing and then using appropriate humor. Think about it—there is always a chance of "bombing" when using your humor. The reasons you might bomb include others not appreciating your humor, others not comprehending your humor, your timing is off, your humor is inappropriate, and so on. However, the more risks you take, that is, the more you try and work to refine your humor and its delivery, the greater the chance of improvement, self-confidence, and success. The fear of bombing or "failure" is the biggest roadblock to creative success. I had a sign in my classroom that said: "Failure should be spelled L-E-A-R-N-I-N-G."

Failure is a vital part of the creative process! You only become better if you try and fail, then learn from your failures. It's just like falling down in skiing or striking out in baseball.

## Where to Get Your Material

Newspapers, magazines, periodicals, and so on, are excellent sources of humor. However, you and experiences in your day-to-day life often provide the funniest and richest material. For example, Bill Cosby once did an HBO comedy special. One of his routines was about a visit to the dentist's office. This one story lasted nearly 15 minutes! This routine is so successful because almost everyone has been to the dentist's office, sat in the chair, and experienced a number of the things Cosby humorously presents. Why do we laugh so? We laugh because he gives us a new perspective, he uses exaggeration effectively, he turns what many people stereotypically find a painful experience into a funny one, and he presents material we can easily comprehend and appreciate.

Think about the common events in your daily routine. A possible daily routine may look like this:

| | |
|---|---|
| Wake up | Lunch |
| Shower | Working/School |
| Breakfast | Going Home |
| Getting to Work/School | Dinner |
| Working/School | |

Additional events may include:

| | |
|---|---|
| Reading the Paper | Holidays |
| Mowing the Lawn | Kids |
| Weekend Activities | Relatives |
| Vacations | |

Get the point? You may have found yourself laughing just now as you read through this "by no means complete" list. Now, if you thought of something humorous just now, take a moment and write it down! This is where and how it begins, by observing and recording (a tape recorder is also a suitable substitute). You can then "rework" and edit the material later.

As you begin to rework daily events and experiences, remember to address the following:

◆ Use of exaggeration.

◆ Add a viewpoint (your viewpoint, others' point of view—kids, neighbor, boss, pets, etc.). Your viewpoint is your unique perspective and your view of the world in which you live.

◆ Elaborate on your attitude as it relates to the event (Were you upset, proud, frustrated, etc.?).

◆ Use of reversal, surprise, contradiction, and incongruity.

## Strategies to
## Facilitate Production of Humor

You may believe you cannot easily produce humor. I suggest throughout this book that humor production is a skill which can be developed. Specific strategies follow to facilitate production. You may generalize and adapt them to your situation.

These activities and examples of humor production have evolved from my work during the past five years with high school students in a summer residential university program. I taught a workshop entitled "Humor: Know Laughing Matter." Students attended this three-week workshop for several hours a day.

During the first week the students were in what I called an awareness/exposure mode. They examined, through numerous examples, various forms and genres of humor, both figural and verbal, aimed at developing an understanding of the five elements of humor: identification, appreciation, mirth response, comprehension, and production. The students also discussed the various theories of humor and other cognitive processes related to humor.

During the second week, the students analyzed a variety of forms of humor (cartoons, jokes, puns, riddles, satire, and slapstick) using various media including video tapes of stand-up comics, films, records, television shows, and books. They analyzed the various skills and processes involved in developing each form of humor and "practiced" these through a series of training activities. The students engaged in the following cognitive and affective processes: imagination, brainstorming, observation, classification, interpretation, application, analysis, evaluation, and synthesis.

During the third week, students selected one form (or possibly a combination of forms) of humor and, working individually or in small groups, created humorous products. The products included stand-up comedy routines, television skits, radio skits, storybooks, cartoon strips, "Top 10" lists, "Brains," cartoon captions, and stories with puns. These products were displayed and shared with the entire group of students attending the class via live performance. Some of the students then elected to participate in the closing talent show, after further refining their humorous entries. This section will demonstrate through student examples how you and your students can intentionally produce humor.

## 1. "Top 10" Lists

With the popularity of "Late Night with David Letterman," the students are very familiar with the nightly Top 10 list. I simply ask each student, or group of students, to create a Top 10 list related to something they and their high school colleagues might appreciate. They usually choose a topic and then generate 15 or 20 possible items. The items are then edited and ranked. The following are examples from the students:

➤ **Example 1—**
**Top 10 Excuses in Baseball**

10. The sun was in my eyes.
 9. I thought he was going to catch it!
 8. It took a bad bounce.
 7. The wind got hold of it.
 6. I wasn't wearing a cup.
 5. I missed the sign, coach!
 4. It was a bad throw!
 3. It was raining.
 2. I thought there were *two* outs!
 1. The umpire's *blind*!! ◄

---
> ➤ **Example 2—**
> **Top 10 Excuses for Unfinished Homework**
---

10. My dog ate it.
 9. My cat used it in her litter box.
 8. My little sister flushed it down the toilet as a science experiment.
 7. It burned, along with my house.
 6. It fell in the mud and you can't read it.
 5. That bully beat me up on the playground and took it.
 4. The wind blew it out of my hand and now it's "Gone With the Wind."
 3. We were robbed last night! They didn't get the VCR, but they did take my homework.
 2. My Dad accidentally used it to start a fire in our fireplace.
 1. What? What homework? I didn't hear you assign anything! ◄

Other examples include:

◆ The Top 10 reasons why we lost the homecoming football game.

◆ The Top 10 reasons the senior prom should not be held in the school gym.

◆ The Top 10 surprises on the school cafeteria menu.

## 2. Cartoon Captions

For this activity, I take 15 *Far Side* cartoons by Gary Larson and cut off the captions. I then ask the students to draw their own captions for the cartoons. Due to the immense popularity of the *Far Side*, many of the students have seen at least one or two of the cartoons, but I challenge them to create a new caption anyway. An interesting note on this activity is that the students often key in on features of the cartoon less important given Larson's original caption. For example, if there is a mirror in a tree, the students might think it is a briefcase instead, and then build the humorous caption around the briefcase. Larson's work is preferable to use with the students due to the fact the cartoons are of the single panel variety, and for a beginning activity, the students prefer them to multiple panel strips like *Beetle Bailey* or *Blondie*. The students also comment how much they enjoy this activity because they do not have to be able to draw.

## ➤ Example 1

The *Far Side* cartoon is one with a Mother and Father greeting someone at the door, and their two children are sitting in front of the television. There are really only 1½ boys, and the caption reads, "Bob and Ruth! Come on in . . . . Have you met Russell and Bill, our 1.5 children?" (From *The Far Side Gallery 3*—see References).

When this cartoon was presented to a group of students, they generated the following captions:

- ◆ "It's okay to come in now. Bob sold the chain saw."
- ◆ "Look! Proof! Nintendo does eat brain cells!"
- ◆ "Look, Dr. and Mrs. Smith. DNA replication right here in our own home!"
- ◆ "And that's Joey's half-brother!"

I have shared this example with numerous groups at conferences and workshops, and without fail, the caption, "And that's Joey's half-brother" brings down the house with laughter. To think a caption for a cartoon, created by a tenth-grade student from Wyoming, was thought to be funnier than Larson's original. ◄

## ➤ Example 2

The *Far Side* cartoon is one with a lobster being plucked from a container of water by a chef and being taken to a steamer on a stove. Larson's caption is, "Auntie Em, Auntie Em. There's no place like home, there's no place like home!" A tenth-grade student created the caption, "What do you mean this isn't a hot tub party!"

As you can see from these examples, this activity allows students to be creative without having to start from scratch. They can choose to use certain visual cues already present in the drawings. Any single panel cartoon will work for this activity. ◄

## 3. Brains

One of the most unique and rewarding examples of humor I have used with students and adults is an activity called "Brains." This idea is really a satire of the recent brain research involving brain hemisphericity. In other words, conventional wisdom and research states the left side or hemisphere of the brain is responsible for logical, rational, intellectual, convergent thought, while the right side or hemisphere is credited as the emotional, sensual, intuitive, divergent side of the brain. The right side of the brain remembers the face, but not the name, and is believed to be the seat of our artistic talent. I thought it would be funny to actually take this notion of a "mental dichotomy" a step further and look at the right and left brains of individuals or groups of people. Hence, the following instructions and examples for the "Brains" activity:

## ➤ Instructions

Whether working individually, with a partner, or in a group, use the following "Brainstorming" process (for an example of a pun, see chapter 2):

A. Brainstorm "Who"—examples of whom to do a "brain" of include individuals (a famous singer or movie star, the President, your local mayor, etc.) or a group of people (volunteer firemen, school principals, high school cheerleaders, etc.).

B. Once a topic for a brain has been chosen, the next step is to brainstorm as many of the following as possible:
   - ◆ characteristics
   - ◆ prejudices
   - ◆ stereotypes
   - ◆ attributes
   - ◆ sayings attributed to the character(s)
   - ◆ events attributed to the character(s)

This is an interesting process. Using the standard brainstorming technique of deferred judgment, students often become involved in exciting discussions about the merits of generalizations, saying things like "you can't say that!" and so on. This is a good opportunity for the teacher to guide the discussion.

C. Once the list of brainstormed stereotypes, events, sayings, etc., has been generated, the next step is to decide if each statement is more appropriate for the right brain or the left brain. At this point, it is also necessary to decide on the proportion of the brain to be allotted for each statement. (Remember, exaggeration generally induces humor and makes a satirical point).

D. Next have the students draw the brains on the handouts provided. They can then transfer them onto clear sheets of acetate by tracing over the original. This allows for sharing of creative products via an overhead projector. ◄

## ➤ Example 1—
## The Brain of an Artist

Let's "dissect" and analyze one of the brains created by a group of high school students and compare it to the characteristics and stereotypes generated. The students decided to look at the left and right brain of an artist.

The left brain contained the following statements:

—"An artist is better than anyone." (A reference to the ego of the artist.)

—"I am ze arteest here!" (A reference to the artist's need for total creative control, as well as a reference to the French as artists.)

—"If I cut off my ear, will she like me?" (A reference to Van Gogh.)

—"What a beautiful bowl of fruit!" (A reference to a still-life.)

—"Please buy my painting." (A reference to the "starving artist".)

—"She didn't like the ear, so now what?" (A second reference to Van Gogh.)

—"You cannot rush a quality painting." (A reference to artists taking their time.)

The right brain of the artist contained the following:

—A large area of self-described talent, with a small dot representing real talent. (A reference to the self-absorbed nature and self-importance stereotype of the artist.)

—Preference for large, empty apartments. (A reference to studios or lofts.)

—Inability to sell work until after death. (A historical reference to an artists' work not being discovered and valuable until after his/her death.)

—Man's inhumanity to man. (A reference to the human condition and adopted as a philosophy by the artist.)

—Preference for berets, silly mustache, and French accent. (Another reference to the numerous famous French artists.) ◄

➤ **Example 2—**
**The Brain of a Trivial Pursuit Player**

One student created the left and right brain of a trivial pursuit player. The right brain (emotional) was divided into sections with the following statements:

—Kill to win.
—Know it all attitude.
—Do anything to see the answer to the next question.
—"I knew that!"
—Bored out of wits until next turn.
—"I should have known that!"
—Can't accept being wrong.
—Argue point until proved.

The left brain (analytical, logical) was divided into six equal sections with the following labels:

—History
—Arts & Literature
—Geography
—Entertainment
—Science & Nature
—Sports & Leisure ◄

➤ **Example 3—**
**The Brain of Barney**

Another example is a group of students created the left and right brain of Barney, that purple dinosaur on PBS loved by everyone under the age of five. The right brain (emotional) was divided into sections with the following statements:

—"I was on top of the world until those Power Rangers!"
—"I've got to get some new colors soon."
—"One more hug and I swear I'll go on a tri-state shooting spree."
—"Oh, no, I'm on my last nicotine patch."
—"I could kick Big Bird's rear."

The left brain (analytical, logical) was divided into the following sections with the following labels:

—"Those Jurassic Park guys live in Wussland."
—"I swear I never inhaled."
—"Get these ancient kids off my show."
—"When is Mother Goose gonna kick off?"
—"My zipper has been stuck for 43 days!" ◄

## 4. Creating a "Punny" Story

Puns often get a bad rap (or rep). People usually groan or roll their eyes upon hearing (or catching) the pun. Oliver Wendell Holmes, himself a lover of puns, once stated, "A pun is the lowest form of wit." And Oscar Levant countered with, "The pun is the lowest form of humor - when you don't think of it first!"

I like to provide a group of students with a topic, then allow them time to generate a long list of related words or phrases (using the brainstorming method discussed previously) and then write their story. The following are examples from high school students:

### ➤ Example 1—Electricity

The puns are in bold type (with the real words, if necessary, in parentheses):

The students had to do a report for their social studies class. They were having difficulty deciding on a topic.

> "**Wire** (why are) we doing this?" said Mary.
> "**Ohm** (oh) I don't know," said Rob.
> "I guess it's for our study of **current** events," stated Ben.
> "Hey, let's make it really funny so our teacher gets a **charge** out of it!" said Mary.
> "Yeah," said Rob, "We can say it was a very creative **outlet!**"
> "**Watt** (what) do you mean?" said Mary.
> "I'm not exactly sure. Let's just **plug** along and come up with some more good **lines**," said Ben. ◀

### ➤ Example 2—Fish

In this example, I will tell the story, and you see if you can identify the puns (at least ten) throughout the story:

> Once at the bottom of the ocean lived a baby fish named Swimmy. As he got older, he wondered what he might be when he grew up.
> "I think I would like to be a sturgeon," said Swimmy.
> "If you want to be a sturgeon, you'll have to go to school," said his Mother.
> "Just perch yourself here on this rock and I'll tell you just what's involved." She then told Swimmy about her uncle who never went to school and now just worked for scale. He could only wave as the others

surpassed him. His large mouth often got in the
way and he never amounted to much.

Swimmy said, "Wow, that sure is a whale of a tale,
Mom."

"I didn't just tell you this story for the halibut,
Swimmy," said Mother.

"Go to school, study hard, and you might want to sing
a song like 'roe, roe, roe your boat' to get you
through the rough seas."

Swimmy fin-nished school and lived happily ever after
as a top sturgeon. ◄

## ➤ Example 3—Trees

I am not going to include the story for this example. I will,
however, provide you with the students' generated list of words
and phrases, so you can try this one on your own (or give it to
your students):

Types of trees:
   fur
   pine
   spruce
   oak
   palm

Parts of a tree:
   sap
   "out on a limb"
   "barking up the wrong tree"
   "root of the problem"
   trunk
   "leaf (leave) me alone"
   "stop needling me"

Words with "tree" in them:
   "tree"mendous (tremendous)
   "tree"son (treason)
   "tree"t (treat)
   secre"tree" (secretary)
   a pal"tree" (paltry) sum ◄

## 5. Telling Stories and Jokes That Were Funny When You Were 6 Years Old!

This activity is similar to "walking down memory lane." Simply
allow students to work in groups of four or five and let them think
back to when they were six or seven years old. Ask them to talk about
the things they remember were funny. Ask them to try to remember
actual jokes or other forms of humor. Some typical humor forms
generated will include:

◆ Knock-knock jokes

◆ Practical jokes

◆ Riddles

Ask the students to think about why most of these do not seem funny (or as funny) to them now. This can lead into a good discussion of the developmental nature of humor (see chapter 11).

## 6. Creating Stand-Up Comedy

Allow students time to create and then deliver to the class audience a short stand-up comedy routine. An excellent "how to" book on this topic is Judy Carter's *Stand-Up Comedy—The Book* (see "Additional Reference Books").

## 7. Creative Cartooning

Have students create their own cartoon or comic strip. An excellent resource is the video entitled Blitz Cartooning (see "Additional Reference Books"). After practicing cartooning with the video, allow and encourage students to create a character and then caption the cartoon.

So, as you can see, it is possible to produce humor with a little help and encouragement. Previous chapters contain numerous examples, strategies, and activities that may allow you to continue to appreciate, identify, and produce humor. What's stopping you? Give it a try!

# Research on Humor Production

Many studies have been conducted during the last twenty years related to the mirth response, comprehension, and appreciation of humor. Little has been conducted on the production of humor by children and adolescents. Masten (1986) conducted a study which examined appreciation, comprehension, and production of humor by 10–14 year old students. The humor production was assessed via the students providing a caption to some cartoons and funny titles to others. The creative titles and captions were then rated on a 0–5 scale by independent judges. Enhanced humor production, comprehension, and greater mirth are often associated with both academic and social competence. Children expressing these humor abilities are often viewed by teachers as more effectively engaged in the classroom and are more attentive, cooperative, responsive, and productive. Their peers often view them as more popular, gregarious, and as more effective class leaders.

When teachers use appropriate humor (and produce humor) in the classroom, there are both benefits and pitfalls. Students are sometimes uncertain and confused as to the teacher's motive for using humor, especially if the teacher uses it infrequently. "Why is the teacher trying to be funny?" This is sometimes seemingly incongruous to the student. "Is the teacher laughing *at* me or *with* me?" "I don't think the teacher's jokes are very funny, but I'd better laugh anyway because I don't want to get on the teacher's bad side. I don't want the teacher to feel bad." Because of the aforementioned concerns, students initially may respond to the teacher's use of humor in the classroom with caution.

There is an additional important benefit of incorporating humor into teaching. Humor encourages a response. Teacher humor may evoke clever responses from the students. The creation of these responses by the students will require both mental alertness and activity. These are qualities to be welcomed in any classroom. In addition to making learning a more enjoyable experience, the use of appropriate humor is a way to change the pace and atmosphere of the class. It has the potential to lessen student apathy. It may be the catalyst toward developing a sense of class cohesion and identity, while simultaneously expressing a positive regard for each student.

Teachers should remember humor is developmental (see chapter 11), and the type of humor children and adolescents respond to and produce is related to their development. It should be noted that individuals in one stage may still comprehend and enjoy humor attributed to previous stages. However, avoid rigidly assigning a stage to a specific age. Each stage can be attributed to an age range from infancy through adulthood.

It is important to remember the relationship of humor development in children and the implications for the teacher in the classroom. Knowing about these stages of development and the types of humor associated with each may be valuable in classroom management and discipline. Practical jokes that occur in the classroom are often disruptive, but the teacher can recognize that these behaviors are consistent with humor development and react accordingly.

The teacher's reaction to the students' production of humor is also something to consider. If a student produces humor in the classroom that is silly or off-color and may be offensive (or even embarrassing) to the teacher or other students, the teacher must remember that the humor often serves some positive developmental purpose for the child. Instead of punishing the child, the teacher might reflect on how these forms of humor address the childrens' concerns, then discuss appropriateness with the student.

I advise you to indicate what and why certain humor is appropriate or inappropriate in your classroom. Your personal values and beliefs, as well as those in your classroom community, must be considered. An open discussion about this can build your cohesive classroom.

In summary, it is important to determine the level of development in your students and the corresponding forms of humor that are typical for their developmental group. Once this is achieved, a) reconsider your reactions to your students humor production, and b) consider proactively (intentionally, purposefully) infusing or including their level of humor into your daily teaching. In short, it is imperative to know your students' "humor level."

## Classroom Activity—Rewrite a Song

In this chapter, we have discussed the importance of humor production and the role it plays in the overall nature of humor. To gain further insight into the element of production, try the following activity. It is designed for use with upper elementary or secondary students in any language arts related class.

**Outcomes:** To allow the students an opportunity to "play" with vocabulary by substituting words in songs.

**Activity:** Use the following example to motivate students to substitute words for a song:

> Propel, propel, propel your craft,
> Placidly down the liquid solution,
> Ecstatically, ecstatically, ecstatically, ecstatically,
> Existence is merely an illusion.

Students should be able to determine this was:

> Row, row, row your boat,
> Gently down the stream,
> Merrily, merrily, merrily, merrily,
> Life is but a dream.

Students may choose any song, poem, fable, or saying and rewrite it using appropriate substitutions. Students can read these aloud and see if anyone can interpret them correctly. New versions can now be used in a book, or, in the case of the song above, sung in a group or a round.

**Classroom Implications:** This activity will help increase the students' higher level thinking skills as well as their creative thinking skills. They must produce appropriate synonyms, then substitute them for the initial words. The behaviors of guessing and risk-taking are also encouraged and enhanced through this activity, involving behaviors necessary to creative thinking.

# Additional Activities Related to Humor Production

1. Modernize (or rewrite in another fashion) fairy tales, myths, or nursery rhymes. It is fun and creative to rewrite the entire work or just the ending. Examples include Cinderella going to the prom on a Harley or Snow White and the Eighth Dwarf.

2. Draw the literal expressions of phrases such as "He really put his foot in his mouth that time," "What's the matter—cat got your tongue?" "She always has her head in the clouds." Also, draw literal words and phrases such as "butterfly" or "He's all tied up right now."

3. Photograph candid shots of the students during various school activities during the week. Ask students to provide captions for each picture. This could be the start of a class yearbook project.

4. Set up a "Tongue-Twister Toughies" station (bulletin board or learning center). Display copies of tongue-twisters. Students can practice these during free time. Allow them to record and graph their fastest times for correctly saying the tongue-twister without errors (more math!) A great spin-off is to allow students to create their own tongue-twisters. Use the dictionary and a thesaurus as a source of possible usable words.

5. Have "Backwards Day." Students and teacher will reverse the day's order, read from back to front, complete worksheets by doing last items first, put some clothing on backward, etc.

6. Infuse appropriate humor in routine internal correspondence. Sometimes a quote or cartoon can get a message across as well as several paragraphs. Once I was elected chair of a college committee, and while preparing the agenda for the initial meeting, decided to attach a cartoon by Callahan. It showed 10–12 people at a conference table, with the caption, "All those in favor of the motion make pirate noises, and all those opposed make horsey noises." During the meeting, the time came for a vote, and all members had a good laugh as they held up the cartoon and pretended to make horsey and pirate sounds. It was a great way to set the informal tone for a committee with major issues to investigate and pursue. I believe I won over several individuals immediately, and minimally we all shared a good laugh.

7. Have the students create their own "Hinky-Pinkies." These are word pairs that rhyme. Students can generate words and clues, such as a lawful bird is a "legal eagle", a comical hare is a "funny bunny", and the robber in charge is the "chief thief."

8. Try creating your own political cartoon (caricature) about a current political or news event. Review the editorial page of your local newspaper, as well as newspaper sections dealing with international/national/regional/local events. Draw a cartoon based on the message intended in an editorial or create your own cartoon related to issues. Provide an appropriate caption for your work.

9. Write your own humorous lyrics to your favorite songs. An excellent master of parody is "Weird Al" Yankovic. Mark Russell has also mastered political parody. A spin-off on this activity is to try to write parodies for poems, stories, or current events. These could be audio taped, video taped, or performed live for the class.

10. Create "Tom Swifties", phrases that use double meanings of words. Begin a bulletin board or learning center and encourage students to add to the following:

   —"Get to the point," he said sharply.

   —"These hot dogs are really good," she said frankly.

   —"Humor is a lot of fun!" he said laughingly.

11. Create original humor buttons, banners, and bumper stickers. Amusing slogans and/or artwork can also be turned into silk screen art for class T-shirts. Caricatures of class members are also a possibility for this product.

12. Design a Rube Goldberg cartoon. These cartoons depict inventions, designed to achieve an incredibly simple task by means of a hilariously complicated scheme, like turning on a light switch or an elaborate alarm clock. Students can use examples and then try to design their own. The process can be compared to that of a computer flowchart.

13. Wordles are puzzles that can represent another word or phrase by their placement. Examples include:

   ◆ ONHOLEE       =       "A hole in one"

   ◆ MAN
     ‾‾‾‾‾
     BOARD         =       "Man overboard"

♦ LAUGH
　LAUGH
　LAUGH
　**LAUGH**　　　=　　　"The last laugh"

♦ **KNEE**
　**LIGHT**　　　=　　　"Neon light"

14. Develop your own comic book or comic strip characters. You may wish to begin by "borrowing" a comic strip character (Charlie Brown, Calvin, Hagar the Horrible, etc.). Work with a partner if you feel you can't draw well. Most materials have writers and illustrators.

15. Look through your family photo album. Use pictures (especially baby pictures) and write conversation bubbles and/or captions. Especially look at the facial expressions in the photographs.

16. Design birthday, get-well, graduation, and other holiday cards with humorous artwork and humorous original verse or brief messages.

17. Have students read and study tall tales. Books about Pecos Bill, Paul Bunyan, and others are available in school and public libraries. An interesting spin-off is to have the students pick a partner, interview each other (perhaps with a predetermined set of questions), and then use the biographical facts to embellish and write a tall tale of each other. Share with classmates. These can be combined into a class book.

18. Allow students to substitute cartooning for written work and reports. The old adage "A picture is worth a thousand words" can apply as students are challenged to creatively illustrate stories, themes, characters, or events. Look for originality and elaboration in the product.

19. Have the students create a "Where in (name of state) are we?" worksheet. Begin with your home state (Let's use Wyoming for an example). Brainstorm a list of clues for cities and towns in the state. A spin-off activity is to allow each student to select a different state or country and create a worksheet using that state's map. Examples from Wyoming are:

♦ Not Pepsiville　　　Cokeville

♦ Bashful girl　　　　Cheyenne (Shy Anne)

- ♦ Friendly ghost        Casper
- ♦ Razor City           Gillette

20. Since every class seems to have a class clown or two, and many teachers seem to have "problems" with their behavior, take away this negative attention by electing or eliciting volunteers to be the "Court Jester" (Classroom Jester) for the week. This student will be responsible to share humor in various fashion throughout the day or during a specific time during the day or week. Another appropriate title might be the "Secretary of Humor."

## Summary

- ♦ "One of the best things people can have up their sleeves is a funny-bone!"
- ♦ "All people smile in the same language!"
- ♦ Three students were working on a parody of a popular song. Several minutes passed and not a sound could be heard from the group. All of a sudden, an explosion, a spontaneous outburst of laughter occurred. I said, "Remember what caused you to all explode in laughter simultaneously—it must have been good!"

These quotations and comments may serve you well in your classroom as you and your students begin to produce and create humor. Remember, the process of producing or creating humor (or anything else) involves risk, so you will need to begin to become a risk-taker. Encouraging your students to take similar risks will be easier if you continue to create an accepting classroom environment where risk-taking behaviors, such as producing humor, are encouraged and rewarded. Remember, "Behold, the turtle. He makes progress only when he sticks his neck out!"

# Infusing Humor into Academic Subject Area Matter: How To's

{7}

To better understand how to intentionally infuse appropriate humor into any academic subject matter in any curriculum, I have decided to use Gagne's (1970) *Events of Instruction* as a framework. These conditions represent the general stages that often must be attained by the learner (with the help of the teacher), usually in the order presented, for learning to effectively occur. The teacher organizes and controls these events. The events are:

◆ Gaining and controlling attention.

◆ Informing the learner of expected objectives.

◆ Stimulating recall of relevant prerequisite capabilities (prior learning).

◆ Presenting the stimuli inherent to the learning task (material).

◆ Offering guidance for learning.

◆ Providing feedback.

◆ Appraising performance.

◆ Making provisions for transferability.

◆ Ensuring retention.

These events of instruction occur in teaching across all academic subject levels and all age levels. They may occur in various combinations, but typically form an instructional situation in the order listed. As we examine each stage in more detail, you can see how easily humor can be intentionally infused.

## Gaining and Controlling Attention

Prior to teaching anything, a teacher must first have the learners' attention. Many teachers look for effective and unique ways to obtain this attention and maintain it throughout a lesson. Sometimes it seems an almost impossible task.

Obtaining and maintaining attention is not difficult, however, it does require some planning and practice. Teachers often use verbal commands like "Now watch this!," "What do you see here?," or "Listen carefully." Gestures, illustrations, and animated techniques can also be effective in obtaining and maintaining attention.

Humor can be effectively employed to maintain attention in a classroom. It can be used singularly or in combination with the techniques mentioned above. For example, I have demonstrated the following technique numerous times before adult and student audiences alike. I simply ask the audience "What goes HA HA HA PLOP?" Then I wait . . . The audience instantly reacts in a variety of ways, all of which maintain attention but act as a prelude to thinking, a catalyst for thinking, and finally result in a number of forms of thinking being initiated. Some in the audience think, "Have I heard this joke before?" (auditory memory). Some try to picture some form of this joke (visual memory). Still others . . . Do I still have your attention? Still others try to figure this out logically (creative thinking and problem solving). Now some in the audience are curious, some are predicting, some are disregarding possibilities they have generated (decision making). Some are even getting frustrated or anxious, because I have still not revealed the answer; But regardless, I still have your attention! Okay. The answer. "What goes HA HA HA PLOP?" "A man laughing his head off!"

I also experience success using cartoons on the overhead projector that relate to a specific topic or subject matter. I don't say anything, I just have the cartoon in place for a minute or two. The laughter of some learners often captures the attention of their peers.

Learners must be attentive to learn. Using humor throughout a class can ensure this, since the learner is never really sure what is coming next! Humor creates anticipation, which, as demonstrated previously, helps obtain and maintain attention. With the desired attention level achieved through the appropriate use of humor, the learners and teacher are linked through enjoyment.

## Informing the Learner of Expected Objectives

The learner must be given information about the type of responses the teacher expects. This provides continuing direction and support in the learning process, and is similar to the popular practice of using advanced organizers. This stage also provides a reinforcement function, as the learners try to match the desired response with those of past experiences, thus knowing if they are correct.

Using humor at this stage will encourage divergent, creative answers. For example, if when teaching a biology lesson involving dissection, the teacher begins by placing the Gary Larson *Far Side* cartoon on the overhead entitled "Planaria sports," with five planaria worms trying to play basketball, and the caption "We're still one player short . . . Someone's gonna have to cut themselves in half." Use of appropriate humor in this situation will aid in creating an atmosphere in which divergent answers are accepted and overtly encouraged.

## Stimulating Recall of Relevant Prerequisite Capabilities (Prior Learning)

Learners must often recall information or concepts previously learned. This learned material often provides a link to present material or is a necessary step in a sequence of learning events. Verbal directions can be used to stimulate recognition of previously learned simple material. Reinstatement is necessary for more complex material.

Humor, both verbal and figural, can aid in this recall process. The saying "a picture is worth a thousand words" applies here, as one cartoon can generate the recall of a great deal of material. It is also possible to assess the comprehension of more complex material by asking students to individually or collectively analyze a joke or cartoon pertaining to the subject matter at hand. For example, the teacher may begin a unit on meteorology by placing a cartoon on the overhead projector showing a weather person in front of a weather map with a pointer, the television camera on, and a caption that reads, "There's a 60% chance of 30% acid rain and a 40% chance of 50% acid rain." The teacher can use this cartoon to elicit the recall of information related to weather maps, the concept of percentages of rainfall, the topic of acid rain, as well as weather predictability and forecasts. Another example might be using the Gary Larson *Far Side* cartoon of a group of our forefathers creating the Constitution with the caption, "So, would that be *us* the people or *we* the people?" This cartoon could be used to assess the prior information of correct English usage and U.S. history.

## Presenting the Stimuli Inherent to the Learning Task (Material)

The stimuli for concept learning is frequently verbal. When we define a concept using words, we are often better able to understand it. This stage is usually achieved by reading. However, with many learners, pictures can greatly facilitate the learning process. Figural humor (cartoons) can sometimes provide the needed visual stimulus to accompany the verbal or written message.

Humor is especially effective when introducing new material. The teacher can use cartoons or other forms of humor to facilitate discovery learning ("What do you see happening in this cartoon?"), ask specific questions related to the academic content presented ("What do you think this means?), or review academic material ("How can you correct this cartoon to make it parallel with what you have learned previously about this topic?"). These examples of infusing humor in this stage will also help facilitate and reinforce the previous events of instruction of gaining and controlling attention, informing the learner of expected objectives, and stimulating recall of relevant prerequisite capabilities (prior learning).

## Offering Guidance for Learning

Verbal instructions are often provided to the learner to achieve guided discovery. Verbal clues are presented to stimulate the recall of information or concepts, then additional cues and questions require learners to discover information and concepts. Most educators adjust the amount of guidance to address the needs of the learner and the context. This guidance can result in enhanced and quickened learning.

Humor can facilitate this learning process. In this case, humor in the form of encouragement can be most beneficial. Sometimes a teacher may ask a humorous question, make a teasing comment, or offer humorous prompts as guidance. Guided discovery may also employ the use of cartoons or other forms of verbal humor. The humor can assist in recall of information or guide the learner in a more appropriate direction. In any case, a benefit of the teacher employing humor is to ease stress and tension. Keep in mind, the reason guidance is offered in the first place is to assist the learner in exploring learning new material, sometimes a threatening experience.

## Providing Feedback

Learning does not just happen. Although some is unintentional (incidental learning), it is mostly intentional, with the learners trying to achieve some level of performance, with either intrinsic or extrinsic motivation and reward. They then want to know the learning was correct. Feedback should be as immediate as possible for learning to be most effective.

Humor can be intentionally used in this process. Both verbal ("Correct," "Not quite," "Super!", etc.) and nonverbal responses (smiles, nods, gestures, etc.) can generally be used by the teacher to assist learners in this process. Enthusiastic, humorous, yet sincere feedback is also a powerful and effective positive reinforcer.

# Appraising Performance

We test, test, and test in public school classrooms to evaluate information acquisition and retention of information and concepts by our students. Multiple choice . . . True/False . . . Fill in the Blank . . . Matching . . . Essay. . . . These traditional methods of assessment provide limited feedback to the learner. Learners often are asked to check their level of understanding and proficiency against an external standard. These tests become a form of motivation to some learners, the bane of existence for others.

I have examined the possibility of using figural (cartoon) humor as an alternative assessment form (Shade, in press). The assessment options previously mentioned are convergent in nature; the question asked by the teacher demands a single, correct response by the student. Although the essay option may initially seem somewhat divergent (open-ended), teachers often develop a "scoring guide" for the essay (points awarded for each concept addressed), and therefore these predetermined "correct answers" make the essay a convergent testing format.

Enter the cartoon. Meaning can be created in the way a teacher structures and then presents information to learners. For example, meaning may be derived from associations existing among and between events, ideas, or objects. Meaning can also be acquired through the associations that exist between a student's past experiences and the material to be learned. The student must be aware of these various associations for meaning to occur. Humor that is contextual and concept or academic subject related may assist in producing such awareness in students. Humor may allow the material to be structured in various and unique ways. This structuring helps students make the necessary associations among ideas as well as to see the various associations that exist between classroom material and their own past experiences. Thus, curricular-related humor may be employed to create the meaningfulness necessary for effective learning.

The use of humor as an alternative assessment may allow for the generation of more divergent answers to questions; recalling and restructuring information in unique ways. Humor may act as a catalyst and allow for unusual juxtapositions and connections to be made between various items of information. Therefore, it may enhance the storage of information by providing a necessary context into which seemingly unrelated items can be better organized. Humor may also increase the information retrieval process by providing specific, easy-to-remember retrieval cues that can be stored along with material to be learned.

Humor also allows separate items of information to be related on different levels. An increased number of cognitive associations can then be made within classroom material. By increasing these associations between material to be learned and material a learner already knows, humor can increase the meaningfulness and integration of new material.

Can the use of humor in the assessment process enhance creative and divergent thinking? Humor may facilitate the expression of a particular mode of thinking so the learner will not be bound to a "right" or a conventional answer. Traditional education is often criticized by many modern educators for the almost exclusive encouragement of the use of convergent thinking in our curriculum. Divergent thinking can certainly be helpful and essential in the educational process involving problem solving, thinking skills, creativity, and activities involving self-expression.

Visual, figural, and auditory humor, like various forms of verbal humor, require a juxtaposition of incongruous ideas. Once presented, the learner must rely on a moderate amount of content to adequately comprehend then respond to the incongruity. Although it may seem bizarre to suggest someone can learn chemistry or physics solely from cartoons, it is not too far fetched to believe a cartoon may focus the student's interest on some scientific issue. Once focused, the interest can be the springboard for gaining an in-depth insight into a new concept.

Instead of asking the question "How much science do you need to know to appreciate science cartoons?", we might better ask "How much science can we learn from cartoons?" The cartoon is a special form of humor where a few squiggles and lines create in the mind of the viewer the image of incongruity that can evoke a smile or laugh. The cartoon builds on the learners' prejudices and preconceptions.

The use of humor as a instructional strategy for teaching and learning is only now being investigated. Teachers with a sense of humor often use this ability to put learners at ease, equalize situations and status relationships, assist learners in finding unexpected connections and insights, as well as increase group rapport among learners.

## Making Provisions for Transferability

Once learning has occurred and skills and concepts acquired, it must be applied or used. The application of learned skills is necessary to demonstrate relevance and provide continued motivation. For example, the main goal of science education is not the rote memorization of a specific principle or formula, rather the application of this knowledge to unique real-life situations. Therefore, it is essential the

teacher provide opportunities to allow for the transfer or gener-
alizability of learning to everyday activities.

The transfer of learning can take place in a variety of ways and
settings. Humor can prove an important outlet in this process. For
example, learners might illustrate a history research paper using at
least three political cartoons. The learners can select (or draw their
own) three political cartoons, with one cartoon related to the main
historical figure and the other two representing both sides of a
political issue. A second example could be to revise the Periodic Table
of Elements. Students can select one of the 109 elements in the
Periodic Table and create a play on words for the element. For
example, Barium—"What you do when CPR fails!"

Another approach to ensure transferability of learning is to ask
students to "correct" the incongruities in a cartoon. For example, a
cartoon might have two dinosaurs in the background that were not
alive during the same geological time period. "Correcting" the cartoon
has the downside of removing the humor. Hence, if the student
"corrects" the humorous product, it should no longer be humorous!

## Ensuring Retention

The amount of practice during the initial learning of information,
skills, or concepts, and relating new information to previously existing
information and experiences, are the best methods for insuring
retention of new knowledge. This is often accomplished by anchoring
new information.

Sometimes the visual clues of a cartoon triggers information that
has previously been anchored in memory. For example, the Bob
Thaves *Frank and Ernest* cartoon about a computer salesman showing
Frank and Ernest a computer and saying, "Now this one has a lot of
storage capacity—256 K plus room for pop, chips, and dip up here"
can help learners as a visual and verbal anchor, allowing them to
recall information about the care of or "do's and don'ts" about
hardware and software care.

Another verbal example is to use the following poem in a
chemistry class:

> Here lies the remains of Henry Low,
> With us he is no more.
> For what he thought was $H_2O$,
> Was $H_2SO_4$.

Discussion of this poem can aid learners in anchoring information
and relating new information to previously existing information and
experiences.

# Summary

Should any of the previous stages be omitted, or even take place out of sequence, learning still occurs, however, perhaps with greater difficulty. Teachers must prepare for the act of learning; this is known as instruction or teaching. As I have demonstrated through numerous examples humor in its various forms can play a role in instruction and learning. The use of appropriate instructional humor seems to enhance learning. It does not alienate, subvert, or deride the educational experience, as some would have us believe. Classroom laughter may initiate and liberate thinking, reduce academic anxiety, promote the retention of academic material, and increase learner satisfaction (additional benefits are detailed in chapter 10).

A sense of humor is one of the most important qualities of a good teacher. The appropriate use of humor in the classroom can serve to keep learners attentive because they are never really sure what may happen next. As demonstrated in this chapter, humor also has the potential to assist both the learner and the teacher in specific instructional processes.

# Action Plans: Classroom-Tested Ideas

The following are more actual classroom-tested, humor-related activities designed to intentionally infuse humor into the classroom. I have developed and presented a number of humor workshops in which participants were instructed to complete a Humor Action Plan (see appendix). The plan includes name, address, and phone number, a plan title, the goals, outcomes, and objectives, a brief description of the plan and how it will be implemented, formal and informal measures of assessment, as well as a tentative timeline. Notice these humorous activities encompass nearly all academic content areas. The following are versions of some of the plans submitted to me during these workshops.

## Language Arts

### 1. Letter Puzzlers

**Outcome:** Students will practice and expand their vocabulary in this fun exercise of divergent thinking.

**Activity:** Build on a letter to make a word:

| | | |
|---|---|---|
| What comes after L? | Bow | (elbow) |
| What comes after E? | Z | (easy) |
| What comes after B? | 4 | (before) |
| What letters explode? | (TNT) | |

Use a different letter each day/week.

### 2. Idioms

**Outcomes:** To see the humor in literature and to explain the difference between idioms and the literal meaning of words.

**Activity:** Read *Morris the Moose* (see References). Discuss how Morris took the expressions literally (e.g., "My nose isn't running, my nose is walking."). Brainstorm other expressions with a literal meaning. Create a class book. Each child can illustrate an expression or idiom and then write the literal meaning (e.g., "It's raining cats and dogs"; illustrate with cats and dogs falling from the sky; it literally means it's raining very hard). Then bind the book and allow parents to sign it out to read at home.

## 3. Onomatopoeia Pie

**Outcomes:** To read and recognize onomatopoeia (a silly-sounding word) and to use it in writing.

**Activity:** On a permanent bulletin board, place a large drawing of a pie. Share with the students examples of onomatopoeia; "buzzing," "squeak," "boom," and other words of this nature. Have the students write the words on cards shaped like apple slices, strawberry slices, etc. Then the students can put the words into the pie. Encourage the students to bring in words found from outside reading. Set aside time in class for students to announce examples, or give them the "license" to spontaneously announce their onomatopoeia anytime they discover or notice it occurring. Perhaps even use an "applause meter" when a student shares a new finding. How many examples can the students find during the year?

## 4. The "Cut-Ups" Class Book

**Outcome:** To have students write a humorous "adventure" story to share with the class. Characters can be the students' best friends who get into predicaments and find humorous solutions. Have students write incidents that happened to classmates throughout the school year.

**Activity:** Read a number of James Marshall's *Cut-Ups* series (see References). Brainstorm similar classroom situations that occurred during the school year. Another twist is to have a "roast." Have the students write and edit each others' work involving situations that were creatively solved using humor.

## 5. Pete & Repeat

**Outcome:** To have students substitute verbs and encourage creative humor in their writing.

**Activity:** Read poems to the class from authors like Shel Silverstein and Jack Prelutsky (see References). Print out the poems with all verbs removed and blank spaces substituted. Allow the students to create new poems with the replacement of new verbs. Share these new creations with the class.

## 6. Joke of the Week Contest

**Outcomes:** To provide students with a "no stress" opportunity to give a short oral presentation before a group of peers; to help students experience some enjoyment in speaking to an audience.

**Activity:** Each student will present one joke or riddle per week to the class every Friday. The student may read the joke, give it from memory, or use a note card. After several weeks or months of these presentations, the teacher could arrange to videotape these sessions. Students could view themselves and provide each other with helpful feedback. The teacher can watch the students to see if overall speaking ability, confidence, and self-esteem improves for each student.

## 7. Wacky Paragraph

**Outcome:** To practice and improve vocabulary.

**Activity:** Write a paragraph using a number of humorous or "wacky" definitions for the given vocabulary words. Have students match or substitute the vocabulary words for the "wacky" phrases. For example: Vocabulary words = shipwrecked, island, tropical.

In 1800, two young men and an old pirate were *boat crashed* in the middle of the ocean. They ended up on a *hot, humid, drizzly teeney-weeney spot of land* miles from nowhere.

Students can substitute the vocabulary words for the humorous phrases.

# Home Economics

## Crazy Meal

**Outcomes:** To give parents the opportunity to visit their childrens' classroom; a chance for students to laugh with their parents; to demonstrate basic reading skills.

**Activity:** Have students create a menu where "made-up" words replace actual words; e.g., spaghetti = narx, fork = plizy, and so on. Invite parents to school where students have prepared the meal. Have students take their parents' orders from the menus in three stages (a three-course meal). Of course, the parents don't know what they're ordering from the silly menu! Possibilities: One parent receives spaghetti, juice, and a knife. Their second course includes dessert, a roll, and a napkin, and the third course is salad, spoon, and a fork. Take everything away after each course. Have students write thank you notes to their parents for attending and being good sports!

# Science

## 1. Revised Periodic Table of Elements

**Outcomes:** For students to become more knowledgeable of the Periodic Table of Elements; for students to see the fun side of science.

**Activity:** Students can work individually or with a partner to select one of the 109 elements in the Periodic Table. They will then create a play on words for the element. E.g.: Barium - "What you do when CPR fails!" Include the atomic weight, atomic mass, and abbreviation. Collect all samples and create a new chart.

## 2. Mirror Mirror

**Outcome:** For students to practice both leading and following.

**Activity:** Students pair up and stand about two feet apart facing each other. One volunteers to be the leader and the other the follower. The leader begins to move his/her hands, then possibly makes facial gestures, and finally a combination of movements. The follower tries to simultaneously duplicate the movements in mirror fashion. Laughter usually occurs both when mistakes are made and when students successfully "mirror" each other!

# Physical Education

## Human Knot

**Outcome:** The students will hold hands in a circle and then "tangle" themselves into a human knot. Instructions to each other to untangle the knot will be given in a foreign language.

**Activity:** Students will get in a circle (10–12 students per circle works best). Students must hold hands throughout the activity. When the teacher says "Go," the students are to tangle themselves (while still holding hands) so as to form a human pretzel or knot. When the students are sufficiently tangled, their task is to untangle themselves. However, they may only speak in a foreign language (e.g., Spanish). The students must be able to successfully use the Spanish words for various body parts, as well as the imperative forms of the verbs necessary to untangle the knot. Students may decide to appoint one person the leader who will singularly give directions to individual classmates in the foreign language. This activity is also challenging and a great deal of fun when used nonverbally.

# Math

## Shrinking Shape

**Outcome:** Students can practice skills of geometry, prediction, estimation, and risk taking.

**Activity:** Using masking tape, place a large shape (circle, square, rectangle, triangle, etc.) on the floor. Ask students if they think all members of the class could stand inside the shape. Usually on the first try, all can fit. Then ask if everyone could fit if the shape was reduced in size. Reduce the size about 5 percent. Now try to fit all class members into the shape. Keep reducing the shape area about 5 percent each time and enjoy the results. Depending on the ages of the students involved, certain "touching" rules might need to be in effect.

Discuss estimation, predictions, guessing, risk taking, and geometry-related issues with the students.

# Social Studies
# or World History

## Cartoons for Conflict Resolution

**Outcome:** To use humor as a catalyst for exploring options to more creatively solve conflicts.

**Activity:** Show students any cartoon depicting some form of violence (Garfield slugging Odie, Dagwood crashing into the Mailman, Calvin throwing a snowball at someone, etc.). Have the students act out the comic scenario (role play) or use puppets. Discuss what happens in the scenario, how the different characters involved feel, and how the reader or audience feels. Brainstorm alternative options for the characters. Replay or rewrite the comic scenario using the newly generated options. This activity provides a good opportunity for students to discuss whether a situation is really funny if it hurts someone. It also provides students the opportunity to generate alternative solutions to real life problems through the process of brainstorming.

# Art

## Class Caricatures

**Outcome:** To allow students the opportunity to draw and learn the technique of exaggeration as a form of humor.

**Activity:** Take instant camera photos of class members, teachers, staff, and the principal. See if students can first verbally describe the features of each subject. Next, verbally exaggerate all features. Now compare the drawings to the verbal exaggerations. Discuss the technique of exaggeration in the drawing of caricatures. Allow each student the opportunity to draw the caricature of someone in the class or school. Collect as examples newspaper and magazine caricatures of national public figures to develop and maintain an interest by students in current events and affairs. Class or school caricatures can be collected for a book, photographed for a year book, or even transferred to T-shirts for class members.

# Any Academic Subject

## 1. Joke or Riddle of the Day

**Outcome:** Students will analyze and discuss why a joke or riddle is humorous.

**Activity:** Each day (or class period) write a joke or riddle on the black board (or bulletin board). Students may use any free time during the day (or class period) to read and answer the item. At the end of the day (or class period), answer, analyze, or discuss the joke or riddle. Especially discuss why the item is funny or why someone else might think it is funny. Jokes and riddles can be related to subject matter or holidays.

## 2. Tell Me a Joke

**Outcome:** To allow children to become more creative and humorous in the classroom.

**Activity:** When the students want to be the one to be "line leader," pass out materials, or any number of other classroom "chores" or events, they must either tell a joke to the class or answer a riddle from the teacher. This can be done every day or maybe one day a week.

## 3. Bulletin Board Bylines

**Outcomes:** To utilize more humor in the classroom by involving students in the production of humor; to allow the students the opportunity to develop a greater appreciation of humor.

**Activity:** Each time you introduce a new unit or review for a test (in any academic subject area), put several enlarged cartoons related to the topic on the bulletin board. Remove any captions. The students are to create captions for the cartoons. Students may work individually or with a partner. Captions will then be displayed. Students may vote on the most creative or funny caption. Be sure to acknowledge and discuss all captions.

# Summary

The previous activities are designed to intentionally infuse more humor into the classroom. However, one practice you as a classroom teacher might want to adopt is to keep a small notebook at hand to record naturally occurring humorous incidents. For example, one day I was explaining a planned project to a group of elementary students. I asked the students to have the product involve "mixed media." I then asked if there were any questions before they began their projects. There were none. Immediately after the students began working, I heard one student ask another, "What did he mean by using mixed media?" The other responded, "You know - how big it should be. Small, media, or large."

At the end of the day read and reread your notebooks of humorous incidents. Sometimes we all experience days where our sense of humor is the only thing that "keeps us going" or "gets us through" the day. I have personally discovered a sense of humor and the ability to laugh at situations and myself often puts both my personal and professional life in perspective. It allows me to achieve balance.

# Caveats When Using Humor in the Classroom

Although we often do not think of it this way, America's classrooms are both academic and social institutions. Teachers spend a great deal of time (some would argue in almost equal proportions) teaching academic content (academic institution) and managing behavior (social institution). This book primarily espouses the benefits of using appropriate classroom humor intentionally to aid in the academic process. However, this chapter not only addresses cautions a teacher should adhere to when dealing with academic content, but also speaks to various ways humor can be used in the social situation of school and the accompanying caveats.

As you contemplate how and when you might use appropriate humor in your classroom, you may find yourself a bit apprehensive about beginning to use it first thing Monday morning with your students. What some teachers worry about when using a humorous approach (loss of seriousness of intention, diminished respect for the teacher, and reduced task orientation and time-on-task behaviors) simply does not occur if humor is gradually introduced, intentionally planned and infused, and mutually enjoyed. If you engage in appropriate classroom humor you are not going to endanger your personal or professional credibility. In fact, in some ways, you may enhance it. I am hopeful, as the title of this book indicates, your apprehensions about using humor in the classroom will be allayed.

## Caveats When Using Humor in the Academic Setting

Using appropriate humor in a purposeful way in the classroom may yield numerous benefits. However, as with most things in life, the benefits are accompanied by potential costs. These must be seriously considered and will vary in type and degree in every classroom. The following are forewarnings or cautions about using humor in an academic setting:

◆ **Distractions**—Any distraction from the learning goal is detrimental to the learning process. Humor not directly related to content is often distracting. For example, sometimes teachers report adding a cartoon at the top of a test in an honest attempt to reduce test anxiety. What often happens is the reverse. The cartoon, if not content specific, is most often viewed by students as a distraction, which increases test anxiety!

◆ **Hostile Humor**—The use of the following forms of humor may be indicative of poor self-image, poor group dynamics, boredom, or misunderstanding; they are all forms of "hostile" humor. These forms of humor are often non-productive and punishing to all involved. They often are indicative of feelings of superiority, that is, putting someone else down or feeling good at the expense of another. Teachers, as well as students, should discourage the use of these forms of humor wherever and whenever they occur.

◆ **Ridicule**—"to mock or make fun of" (*Webster's Dictionary*). This is similar to the modern notion of "put-downs" (the belittlement of others). Previously, teachers have used humorous ridicule as an educational corrective. This has been shown to be very ineffective for preschool children, and not much better for older students, probably due to the accompanying indirect and veiled messages being too ambiguous for young children. This form of humor as a corrective should only be used when the ends can justify the means, and then, sparingly. Although an immediate behavioral change might occur when using this form of hostile humor, the long-term costs of diminished self-esteem may outweigh any short-term benefits.

◆ **Satire**—"literary composition holding up to ridicule vice or folly of the times; use of irony, sarcasm, invective, or wit" (*Webster's Dictionary*). Satire is concerned with the nature of reality. It emphasizes what seems to be real but is not. The essence of satire is the revelation of the contrast that exists between pretense and reality. Satire, then, is a comic device used to criticize and ridicule. Satire, irony, and puns are sometimes described as "higher" forms of humor. They often involve symbolism, and require the prerequisites of advanced language abilities and comprehension of the material in question. Therefore, they have the potential to misinform the learner. Teachers must know their students well enough to know if they will "understand" the intended humor of satire, irony, and puns and be able to make the necessary cognitive corrections. The teacher must decide whether to discuss material prior to, during, and/or following the presentation of this type of humorous material. Otherwise, distortions and misinformation will prevail, even though unintended.

◆ **Cynicism**—"disbelief in goodness" (*Webster's Dictionary*). The cynic believes mankind's behavior is based on self-interest. Someone who is cynical is often distrustful of the motives of others.

◆ **Sarcasm**—Sarcasm is brutal. Even the word itself has an appalling root meaning - from the Greek *sarkasmos*, to tear flesh! Self-esteem is invariably wounded by the use of this knifing form of wit. However, students should be taught how to recognize and analyze sarcasm, and it should be suggested to them they should avoid its use. Sarcasm humiliates, mocks, and makes fun of its victims and immediately puts them on the defensive, often leading to poor attitudes and deep resentments.

## Categories of Humor to Avoid

I previously discussed numerous categories of humor. Whether you personally find these "types" of humor funny or not, many of these categories should probably not be addressed or used in the school environment. These will be briefly described here (for a more detailed description of each category, please refer to chapter 2, "Identification"):

◆ **Sexual**—Jokes celebrating the fun of sex, mildly flirtatious to outright obscenity and lewdness.

◆ **Ethnic/Racial**—Jokes in which a particular ethnic group is demeaned, ridiculed, or made fun of.

◆ **Religious**—Jokes making fun of particular religions or religion in general.

◆ **Hostile**—Jokes in which an attack on someone's dignity is the primary focus. These may be insulting, invective, or involve a put-down of someone.

◆ **Demeaning to Men/Women**—Jokes in which males/females are discredited or put-down, often by the opposite gender.

◆ **Sick**—Jokes making fun of death, deformity, disease, or handicapping conditions.

As you can understand, these categories of humor are rarely appropriate in a school environment; their use should be avoided by teachers, and teachers should also discourage the use of these categories of humor by students. Such categories of humor reflect bad taste or poor judgment.

## The Absence of Humor

Interestingly, the apparent absence of humor in an individual student or in groups of students may indicate any of the following: high levels of anxiety, low levels of communication, low cohesiveness, reduced productivity, alienation, dissatisfaction, and stress. The perceptive teacher can observe the degree of interpersonal and intrapersonal humor use among students in the classroom in diagnostic fashion, identifying the lack of humor as a "red flag," if any of the aforementioned problems are evident.

# Caveats When Using Humor
# in the Social Setting

One of my favorite humorous stories related to discipline in the classroom is as follows. It seem little Claude's mother had reluctantly allowed her precious son to attend public school. She gave the teacher a long list of instructions on the first day, including, "My son Claude is so sensitive. Don't ever punish Claude. Just slap the boy next to him. That will frighten Claude."

Humor is often used in social settings for a variety of reasons. The affective dimensions of humor use are equally important in the classroom.

## The Class Clown

The class clown exists—Always has, always will—Period. Many class clowns are disruptive—Period. By understanding both the nature of humor and the class clown who employs it, the perceptive teacher can enhance social interaction and communication while reducing classroom disruptions. The use of humor in the classroom may thus be viewed as either an asset or a liability.

"I'd give my right arm for a classroom filled with students who are independent, creative, well-accepted, you know, leaders—popular, active, and task-oriented." This phrase has often been spoken by many teachers at some point in their career. These are the same attributes of adults and adolescents who possess wit and humor. Given such positive characteristics as those attributed to the adolescent wit, why is it so many teachers respond so negatively to the "class clown?"

One possible answer to this question relates to the issue of control. Since humor is a form of communication, it has both expressive and receptive functions. These aid in behaviors such as the release of tensions, the maintenance of the social structure, and the facilitation of goal attainment. Humor may also have both control and conflict functions. However, in light of this, it should be noted one of the problems in our schools even today is many teachers cannot distinguish between these two kinds of humor. Teachers tend to focus on the conflict functions. Consequently, they seldom see any ways humor can positively control student behavior or maintain the stability of the students' social system. Instead of being viewed as constantly disruptive, humor may offer a means to keep crises to a minimum in the classroom. It may be that punishing the class clown is not entirely appropriate! This chapter offers alternatives to punishing those who generate disruptive behaviors in the classroom.

Remember, the school also acts as a social institution. Is there a place for humor? Fabrizi and Pollio (1987) state, "As long ago as 1932, Justin notes that schools are responsible for 'civilizing' the expression of humor by children, and although this attitude yields a slight suppression of humor for all types, it produces a more focused suppression for directed remarks as children advance from elementary to high school" (p. 124).

## Role of Humor in the School

Although humor, laughter, and smiling are frequently occurring human traits and events, we as a society do not have a clear sense of their meaning and value. I believe this is especially true in education, where humor is seen both as creating a problem for, yet also an advantage to, classroom learning. The usual assertion is that humor often disrupts the classroom environment and may also be a sign of immaturity in children who produce it. Here are several interesting points to consider:

1. The production of humorous events (laughter and smiling) by students often decrease as students get older. This also indicates humor is a relatively infrequent classroom event!

2. Humorous actions of both boys and girls show little difference in the context of the school classroom.

3. For seventh graders, humor is one of many behaviors in need of control—and the teacher regularly does this. As for the 11th graders, humor is associated with being a significant classroom participant who regularly interacts in positive ways with teachers and fellow students.

4. Many students (even those who rarely receive any form of reprimand from the teacher) often avoid producing humor when teachers are present because they have seen teachers routinely reprimand certain students for producing humor and then possibly anticipate similar consequences for themselves.

This is more prevalent with older students who have spent more time in the school system. This suggests that while negative reactions represent the usual response to humor, a few older students are sometimes encouraged in their classrooms to produce humor.

In summary, it should be noted a clearer behavioral answer to the question of how teachers and society in general perceive and interpret the role of humor in the classroom. These perceptions and interpretations provide an understanding of how such perceptions guide what teachers do and how they react to humor created by students of different ages. For most older children (adolescents) humor is responded to by reprimand and other negative reactions. This defines it as an unwelcome behavior in the school environment. Although exceptions are sometimes made for some students, this generalization seems to best summarize the overall attitude of educators toward the use of humor in the classroom.

## Positive Effects of Humor in the Classroom

Only now are many educators beginning to realize the positive effects of using humor in the classroom. As mentioned previously, society views the traditional role of education of the masses to be a social control responsibility. A historical perspective related to the role humor has played in education is that humor in the classroom is a twentieth century phenomenon. Previously, it was considered unscholarly to use humor as a teaching strategy or even to show a sense of humor as a personality trait. Traditional subject matter and accompanying lessons were supposed to keep all students interested. Thus, the prevailing view was (and often still is), that to entertain is not to educate! If there is laughter in the classroom, then learning cannot possibly be occurring.

Humor is often viewed as unnecessary, undignified, and completely contrary to the notion of the serious, classic educational experience. Traditionally, the attitude of teachers toward laughter and humor has been the notion that they are frivolous activities that detracts from what is important, presumably the rote memorization of academic content. This would lead us to the idea that life is basically serious business. If laughter and humor have any place at all it is not in the classroom.

In summary, it appears teachers have historically perceived teaching and learning with a sense of humor as unprofessional, uncontrolled, and undignified. Teachers have even avoided using humor in speeches, social intercourse, and presentations for fear of being thought of as trivial, foolish, or ignorant. Perhaps we inadvertently link humor to mere popularity and likability. Many teachers may make a conscious decision to be "humorless" when teaching because "serious professionals" must conduct their business in a serious manner!

# The Role of Humor in Classroom Management

Discipline is a major problem in American schools today. Discipline is often the leading topic in needs assessments conducted by school districts. Could discipline problems stem from teachers who are not enthusiastic about their teaching? Could it be teachers too seldom provide humor and stimulation in their classrooms?

More laughter and humor in the learning process may be risky, but it has the potential to combat boredom—for the student and the teacher. The class clown and the rebel often have one thing in common—the need for laughter and spontaneity in the learning process. Creativity and rebellion yield distractions and discipline problems. Creativity and humor in an accepting environment can create an atmosphere where learning can flourish!

The teacher is in a position to guide individual students, and the class as a whole, toward appropriate humor, and away from the forms of hostile humor. The class clown's energy can be channeled in a more creative, productive, and appropriate fashion.

What may prove especially helpful to teachers are the positive social functions of humor. Through laughter, class clowns can release tensions, possibly increase the sense of group rapport and cohesion, and permit the deviant behavior of other students without causing loss of face or hurt feelings. Humor may also be an effective communication channel for conveying information about students' feelings and attitudes. Therefore, to respond in a punishing manner to a whimsical class clown may prove counterproductive to the teacher's classroom management plan.

Another extremely simple and effective way to use humor in classroom management is using "intentional mistakes." Making intentional mistakes is perhaps the most underutilized learning technique in teaching today. And it certainly can be humorous as well. It's simple. Just make an intentional mistake while teaching any academic content. Challenge students to identify the mistake. Think of it—they have to pay attention, comprehend, then discriminate and evaluate the nature of the material presented. Once this has occurred, they must take a risk and challenge the teacher, implying the teacher made a mistake.

Risk-taking is an often overlooked skill seldom encouraged in our educational system. Remember, without risk, there is no gain. People who do not take risks constrict their emotional range. Think of the self-confidence at work here. Next a student can be helped to "correct" the teacher's mistake. Humor often results. This strategy also has numerous side benefits, including making the teacher seem more human, increasing student-teacher rapport, and it also gives teachers an invaluable "out" if they make a mistake. The mistake wasn't intentional, and the students think it was because the teacher frequently employs this strategy. Some intentional mistakes can be similar to the old "Fractured Fairy Tales," or stand-up comedian Norm Crosby's routines in which he misuses words. Examples from an algebra class include substituting "friction" for "fraction" and "sex" for "six." This guarantees the students will pay attention and laugh!

## When Humor Doesn't Work!

Not everyone can use humor effectively in the classroom nor to the same degree as another. It depends on a number of variables, including:

◆ your personality.

◆ your tolerance for student-centered versus teacher-centered activities.

◆ your overall ability to maintain an effective classroom management plan and the accompanying procedures.

Another caveat related to the use of humor is using humor as a defense. By this, I mean continually 1) keeping things light and easy, 2) not taking things seriously, 3) keeping oneself at a distance from the feelings or situation through the use of humor, 4) or not admitting something and trying to "laugh it off." The class clown or class comedian is also referred to as a "smart-alec." If someone laughs at what I did or said, they must like me. I have been validated. I might then always try to be funny, because I'm afraid you might not like me or might stop liking me. Humor in this form is really used as a "mask," as we cover up our true feelings as a means of avoiding intimacy with others or try to hide from the reality of a situation.

The following responses from classroom teachers are examples of humor that did not go as expected:

◆ "There have been times when I have told a joke in my classroom, and the kids didn't think it was funny—there was no reaction whatsoever from them. Boy, was I ever embarrassed!" Several things to remember from this example include knowing your students, watching the age level and comprehension levels of your students, and, if you feel bold enough, asking students to "explain" your joke; in other words, why do they think it's funny or not funny.

◆ "Once I started out a class using a joke related to the subject matter. All the kids laughed, however, some thought they had now been given permission for a 'free-for-all.' It took me longer than I'd like to admit to get the class back under control again." I believe humor can most effectively be used once a good classroom management program is in place. As stated previously, humor can distract and give the appearance students are off-task, out-of-control, and not possibly learning anything. The teacher with a good classroom management style and plan can help the students know what types of humor are appropriate in the classroom and what are not, as well as when and how much is acceptable.

◆ Sometimes humor can be misinterpreted by students, especially younger ones. One teacher related the following story. She was going to be married in a few weeks, and, after telling her students the news, stated she had arranged to get a school bus to take all 26 of them with her on her honeymoon. She said she didn't want to leave them for five school days! Some students went home and reported her plans to their parents. Believe it or not, several parents phoned her later that evening to check her story! She said the whole thing was quite embarrassing. The lesson here again is to help your students to understand when you are "kidding" and when you are "serious."

◆ As mentioned in the previous story, many times students do not know for sure when or if you are teasing, kidding, or joking. The perception of the teacher always being serious is a barrier for the teacher and student as one attempts to use appropriate humor in the classroom. It is imperative you know your students fairly well prior to using various types of humor. Also, as a role model and instructor, help them to identify, comprehend, and use appropriate humor in the classroom.

◆ Don't use humor to correct a serious, on-going behavior problem. It has the potential to backfire, and may lead to sarcasm being used by both parties, and that certainly can be destructive. An individual conference may be more helpful.

◆ Don't use humor to try to get a student out of an extremely bad mood. The mood can worsen if the students feels he or she (or the problem) is not being taken seriously. A demonstration of caring support may be more helpful.

# Do's and Don'ts of Using Humor in the Classroom

I have found we as teachers appreciate a list of classroom-tested guidelines as we investigate new methods and techniques. In summary, I offer the following list of "Do's" and "Don'ts" to use appropriate humor in the classroom. These guidelines relate to both academic and social settings.

## Do's

♦ It is often advisable to use self-disparaging humor in the classroom. This form of humor is almost always "safe," as the joke or humor is aimed at yourself instead of the students.

♦ Do differentiate between the two types of class clowns: the sarcastic/hostile and the clowning/whimsical. Remember, they are vastly different in their personalities and the ways their humor is manifested in the classroom. Actions of the clowning/whimsical class clown are usually welcomed as they are often creative and productive. On the other hand, the behaviors of the sarcastic/hostile clown are often unproductive, distracting, and unacceptable. These should be discouraged and substitute behaviors encouraged by the teacher for the benefit of all involved.

♦ Do use intentional mistakes in your daily classroom instruction. This underused teaching strategy will yield numerous benefits.

♦ Do watch for those who may be using humor as a crutch to avoid taking things seriously or to keep their feelings at bay.

♦ Do note the age level and comprehension levels of your students as you begin to use appropriate humor in the classroom.

♦ Do get to know your students well before you try out various forms of humor in the classroom.

## Don'ts

♦ Don't tease without permission! Ask the student privately, "Do you mind if I tease you about . . .?" It is imperative you get to know your students well before attempting teasing of any kind.

◆ Remember, distractions are detrimental to the learning process. Avoid using humor not directly related to academic content.

◆ Hostile humor, including ridicule, satire, cynicism, put-downs, and sarcasm should be avoided in the classroom setting. They are often non-productive and punishing to all involved, often putting someone else down or feeling good at the expense of others.

◆ A number of categories of humor should be avoided in the classroom. These include the following: sexual, ethnic/racial, religious, hostile, sick, and demeaning to men and/or women. These categories of humor reflect bad taste and/or poor judgment.

◆ Given the information related to the class clown, it would seem that punishing this creative individual may not always be appropriate.

◆ Remember, you should be laughing *with*, not at someone. Think of it like this: would you be mad or embarrassed if it happened to you? However, you laugh when the same thing happens to someone else. Let this be a gauge of whether or not something is funny.

◆ Don't use humor to attempt to correct a big behavior problem, and don't use humor to try to get a student out of an extremely bad mood.

## Summary

A final note. It is important to think of both the pluses and the minuses when examining the appropriate use of humor in the classroom. As you ponder both, try to not let the minuses outweigh the pluses. Just know they are there, and deal with them appropriately. Always remember:

An optimist laughs to forget.
A pessimist forgets to laugh!

# Benefits of Using Humor in the Classroom

**10**

Researchers, medical personnel, and educators often espouse the benefits of the use of humor in their respective fields. Both a personal sense of humor and the use of humor in the work environment are essential. Many teachers state their experiences of using humor in their classrooms are beneficial in almost all aspects of the learning process. In contrast, the results of empirical studies on using humor in teaching offer mixed results as to its effectiveness.

A review of the literature provides numerous oversimplifications and contradictory evidence on the intentional use of humor in the classroom as a facilitatory tool. Often, these mixed results and mixed feelings on the subject drive a continuous wedge between classroom teachers and academic scholars of instructional practice. Interestingly, journals that report positive results in the use of humor in the classroom often involve elementary and secondary school subjects. Most insignificant results in studies conducted on the use of humor in the classroom are obtained from investigations utilizing college students as subjects. We are really comparing apples and oranges, i.e., children versus adults and free, compensatory education versus voluntary, paying students. Therefore, let's remember results obtained from one subject group are not necessarily generalizable to another.

As I thought of the challenge of bridging the gap between empirical research and implementation in the field, the title "License to Laugh" came to me soon after I presented a workshop on humor at a national convention in Los Angeles. During the presentation, I said we as teachers often "believe" something works and perhaps has benefits; we "just know." However, we often second-guess ourselves. If we hear about it at a workshop, in-service meeting, or staff development workshop from an "expert" who says it is okay to do it or use it, we then feel validated. I said what was really needed was simple "permission," hence the title, "License to Laugh."

In this chapter, I draw upon research to support the "gut feeling" that humor in the classroom is beneficial. Some students and teachers may benefit (at certain times and under certain conditions) in some or all of the areas described in this chapter. Some might seem more appropriate for use with elementary students, others for secondary students. Some activities will work with all ages. If you elect to use humor appropriately in your classroom, here are some of the things you can expect, in varying degrees, to happen.

## 1. Self-Esteem Enhancement

A positive attitude and a positive self-image can result from a positive classroom environment. Both teachers and students can improve their own self-concepts if they appropriately use humor and share humorous experiences to bring pleasure to each other. Shared laughter is a powerful way to reinforce all aspects of learning. The establishment of such an environment often removes most academic and social barriers to learning. Students are then free to explore, play, and take risks because a form of accepting, group support system that allows for human error and failure is in place. Mistakes, errors, and failures are expected, and therefore, do not become any kind of traumatic experience. The freedom to fail may be one major catalyst of creativity. When dedicated people are given the freedom to fail in their endeavors, their enthusiasm may spark ideas seemingly very fantastic and far out upon first examination.

Humor can also promote and increase a feeling of group membership. As humorous experiences occur and are shared over time, a form of bonding can occur between group members. People laugh louder and longer when in large groups. Have you noticed you often laugh louder and longer when you are with others at a party, the movies, a seminar, a conference, or in a classroom? A sense of security and even increased self-confidence may result from group laughter, as this is almost always an emotionally positive experience.

## 2. Improved Motivation

Everyone can relate to being under pressure and stress. We all know how that feels. At the same time, we have all experienced varying degrees and durations of laughter and the invigorating feeling that follows a good laugh. A physiological explanation exists for this pleasant phenomenon; the chemical substance catecholamine, which actually increases alertness, is produced. Of equal importance are studies showing certain types of cholesterol produced under stress cease to be produced following laughter.

Teachers can use this information to their benefit by using appropriate humor in teaching to obtain and maintain attention and motivation and put students in a more alert state of mind. Interest and motivation can be maintained with the periodic use of content-related humor throughout the lesson.

# 3. Stress Reduction

Stress is ever-present in our society. You will never be rid of it; it cannot be eliminated. However, it can be significantly reduced, and we can learn how to better cope with it. In fact, stress is actually good! For example, look at any room of any building. Do you realize that if there was no stress, the walls could not support the ceiling and it would come crashing down? Stress, or tension in this case, is actually positive and advantageous, depending on how you choose to look at it!

Think about each of the following statements and what implications they have for your life in the workplace, at home, and specifically, in your classroom:

◆ When you laugh your brain discharges hormones that release endorphins, the natural pain-killers in the body.

◆ You can't laugh and be depressed at the same time.

◆ Anxiety can't exist concurrently with the physical state of laughter.

◆ Shared laughter indicates a common perception; it's an instant link to communication; it creates a "comfort zone."

◆ Norman Cousins once asked the question, "If negative emotions produce negative chemical changes in the body, wouldn't the positive emotions produce positive chemical changes?"

◆ Again, from Norman Cousins, "I made the joyous discovery that ten minutes of genuine belly laughter had an anesthetic effect and would give me at least two hours of pain-free sleep."

◆ Laughter is often followed by a state of physical relaxation and reduced physical tension and stress.

# 4. Anxiety (Test) Reduction

Recent research on humor and its pedagogical utility shows humor can help to reduce several types of anxiety in the classroom. This research indicates humor may be a powerful classroom tool to reduce the anxiety that can often accompany the learning process. Humor has been attributed to the facilitation of creativity in the classroom by reducing students' anxiety levels. Reduction in test anxiety when humorous items were included on examinations has also been studied. Humor has also helped some students maintain their attention, it relieves boredom, and reduces overall anxiety in their classroom. Tension and mental fatigue are often created during serious and intense instructional lessons. Attentiveness usually fades and anxiety increases. Humor can be a great remedy for such tension. It can often relax and engage the audience so people will pay attention and be motivated to listen better.

Can classroom teachers utilize the knowledge humor may reduce test anxiety on an on-going basis? Too often, teachers resist the use of a "new technique" because they view it as another add-on for which they have little "extra" time. It is not necessary to view humor as another curricular frill or "add-on". Humor can be instrumental in developing many types of skill and appreciation activities. Humor may represent a more palatable way of teaching many aspects of our current curriculum.

Numerous novel ways to use humor to reduce anxiety in the classroom are discussed in the activities presented in chapters 2–6. For example, cartoons are very easy to use and are easily obtainable. They are easy to control; they should be appropriate to the content, and they must not mock or make fun of students. Cartoons can be used not only during the teaching of academic material, but also on lab assignments and examinations. Cartoons can allow students to see connections between information presented in class and information they need to finish homework and succeed on quizzes or examinations. Using cartoon humor may reduce test anxiety and even encourage students to do homework.

To add further research support to the notion of using cartoon humor in the learning process, Schacht and Stewart (1990) reported "Finally, we chose cartoons as a medium because of their inherent tension-reducing function. The comics act to reduce tension in their readers mainly by offering variety and recurrent focus of interest. Their name implies that they also reduce tension through laughter. Thus cartoons can prevent boredom and can act as a safety valve for students' anxiety" (p. 54).

# 5.  Other Health Advantages

We've all heard the phrase "Laughter is the best medicine." Norman Cousins probably said it more realistically as "Laughter is *good* medicine." The following are health advantages described in the literature as having a positive effect on those who employ it on a regular basis:

◆ Immune System—Recently a number of medical research studies have examined the effects of various forms of humor on the immune system. Our thoughts and emotions (including laughter) affect the immune system by communicating through nerve pathways and neurohormonal transmitters (central nervous system). These transmitters, including endorphins, lymphokines, hormones, interferon, and a host of others, reportedly reduce discomfort sensitivity.

◆ Norman Cousins's much referred to work, *Anatomy of an Illness* (see "References"), describes a now classic account of how the editor of the *Saturday Review* used his own healing powers of courage, tenacity, and laughter to successfully battle a crippling disease known as ankylosing spondylitis. Physicians at the time claimed Cousins had a 1 in 500 chance of recovery. Cousins and his physician decided on a course of action that included massive doses of vitamin C and laughter. He repeatedly watched "Candid Camera" classics and Marx Brothers's films. His nurse would read to him humorous selections from E. B. White and Max Eastman. Positive emotions and laughter seemed to be affecting his body chemistry in a positive way. He eventually fully recovered from the illness doctors had previously described as progressive and incurable. When asked later about the importance of the laughter in his recovery, Cousins stated, "What was significant about the laughter was not just the fact that it provides internal exercise for a person flat on his or her back—a form of jogging for the innards—but that it creates a mood in which the other positive emotions can be put to work, too. In short, it helps make it possible for good things to happen" (Cousins, 1981, pp. 145-46).

◆ Using humor when someone is seriously ill reunites instead of separates. If two individuals share common laughter, it shows how similar, not different they are. As the comedian Victor Borge said, "Laughter is the shortest distance between two people." Seeing a situation in a light-hearted or humorous way may be viewed as another form of support. Recently, newspapers and magazines reported how young cancer patients, who felt very self-conscious and different from their peers due to their loss of hair during chemotherapy and/or radiation treatments, arrived at home or school to find their friends and loved ones had shaved their heads as a show of support and solidarity. The idea here was to make the environment, in this case the classroom, an environment safe for clever, witty, warm, funny stuff. A classroom climate that models and encourages humor may have by-products beyond measure.

## 6. Improving Morale and Team Building

Stop. Look. Listen. We can often find humor in the workplace. Examples of humor in the workplace include jokes and job-related puns, stories related to experiences in the field, anecdotes, and teasing. Benefits often include the creation of a more pleasant work environment and the ability to create bonds among workers which allows them to accomplish tasks more efficiently and effectively. Humor can also have a significant impact on the level of employee satisfaction.

I have selected the following examples of humor from three different occupations (insurance companies, the medical profession, and the teaching profession). These examples demonstrate how humor can be found everywhere within each profession and workplace. These are found in the book *Anguished English* by Richard Lederer (see References).

The following are actual claims reports in the files of different insurance companies:

—Coming home, I drove into the wrong house and collided with a tree I didn't have.

—In an attempt to kill a fly, I drove into a telephone pole.

—An invisible car came out of nowhere, struck my car, and vanished.

—The gentleman behind me struck me on the backside. He then went to rest in a bush with just his rear end showing.

—The indirect cause of the accident was a little guy in a small car with a big mouth.

—I saw a slow-moving, sad faced old gentleman, as he bounced off the hood of my car.

—I pulled away from the side of the road, glanced at my mother-in-law, and headed over the embankment.

—I was on my way to the doctor with rear end trouble when my universal joint gave way, causing me to have an accident.

The following examples are related to the medical profession:

—A doctor's chart report: "On the second day, the knee was better; and on the third day it had completely disappeared."

—Another patient's chart: "Skin: Somewhat pale, but present."

—A report filed by an attending nurse: "The patient was seen by Dr. Smith who felt we should sit on the abdomen, and I agree."

—A discharge report: "Discharge status: alive, but without permission."

The following are excuses received by teachers from the parents of students (or perhaps the students themselves) who had been absent from school:

—"Please excuse Roland from P. E. for a few days. Yesterday he fell out of a tree and misplaced his hip."

—"Please excuse Jimmy for being. It was his father's fault."

—"Please excuse my son's tardiness. I forgot to wake him up and I did not find him till I started making the beds."

Humor can help people improve human relationships. It is difficult for students to "tune out" or "turn off" in class if they can share a humorous moment with their teacher on a daily basis.

Work and school should be fulfilling. Humor appears to create bonds between the employees at all levels and facilitates the completion of tasks. Members of cohesive work groups are more often involved as both the initiator and the focus of humor than those in noncohesive work groups. There is a bonding aspect of humor that may have a significant impact on both the employees levels of satisfaction and workplace productivity.

It would seem these observations could also be applicable to any classroom environment. It is possible for learning to be more enjoyable and less stressful in an environment that encourages and acknowledges appropriate classroom humor.

An interesting aside; the astute teacher might use the knowledge of humor as a diagnostic device. The absence of humor in a small group might indicate poor bonding, morale, or teamwork. This could eventually result in a poor performance by the group as demonstrated by decreased productivity or individual dissatisfaction.

## 7. Enhancing Creative Thinking

Laughter can free the mind from fixed mind sets and paradigms. The phrase by Arthur Koestler, "Ha-Ha can lead to Ah-Ha!" is often used and documented in the literature on creativity. Humor promotes an increase in creativity.

Humor can also put a problem in proportion so it can be better managed and then solved. Humor can also create the much-needed distance between yourself and the problem to be solved. If you are totally absorbed, it is harder to create a new attitude and effect a solution.

## 8. Enhancing Divergent Thinking

Closely related to creativity is divergent thinking. Many believe humor can act as a catalyst and open the door to further creative and divergent thinking. Humor may allow for unusual juxtapositions to be made between various pieces of information. Therefore, it may enhance the storage and subsequent retrieval of information by providing an appropriate context into which apparently unrelated items can be filed and organized. Humor can enhance the retrievability process by providing distinctive, easy-to-remember retrieval clues that can be stored with any material to be learned. It therefore increases the number of relevant cognitive links, or associations, that can be made within academic subject material. If we can increase the number of these associations between material a student already knows and new material to be learned, humor may facilitate an increase in the meaningfulness of new material and therefore enhance the learning of such material.

Can the use of humor in the evaluation process enhance creative and divergent thinking? Humor facilitates the expression of a mode of thinking not bound to "right" or conventional answers. Although content knowledge is currently doubling every 18 months, public schools continue to encourage the use of convergent thinking in classrooms at the exclusion of divergent thinking. However, divergent thinking is necessary for effective creative problem solving and higher level thinking skills.

The use of cartoon humor has additional benefits in enhancing divergent thinking. Meaning is created in the way a teacher structures and presents information to learners. Appropriate, concept-related humor may play an important role in producing such meaningful learning. Humor may allow material to be constructed in unique or unusual ways. This structuring and restructuring may help students make necessary associations among ideas. They may also be able to see associations that exist between their own experiences and the newly presented classroom material. The use of appropriate humor related to the curriculum may be used to create the meaningfulness necessary to facilitate effective learning. In addition, the use of humor as an alternative assessment may allow for the generation of more divergent answers to questions; recalling and restructuring information in unique ways.

## 9. Avoiding Burnout

Burnout is often described as adverse psychological, behavioral, and/or physiological reactions to excessive occupational stress. Depending on the specific work environment, burnout can be caused by factors such as role conflicts, personal conflicts, an excessive workload, persistent crises, and seemingly little control in personal and professional decision making. Humor can aid in changing the perception of the stressful situation. The situation can be viewed as not so overwhelming: stimulating versus threatening and challenging versus problematic.

Any of us in the "helping" professions: teachers, doctors, nurses, lawyers, counselors, social workers, firefighters, police officers, etc., have the potential to sometimes fall victim to the emotions and feelings of our students, clients, and patients. To be effective, we must be emotionally able to distance ourselves from the situation: empathetic versus sympathetic, objective yet maintaining a degree of compassion. Laughter can help maintain our personal strength. Privately, we can use humor both defensively (passively) as a coping strategy and offensively (actively) to lighten up and possibly better manage stress. It is important to remember never to use this humor in front of those we are trying to help.

Using humor in our daily lives and in our professional working environments offers several benefits. The first is the maintenance of positive energy (from emotions such as laughter, joy, and hope) which makes us stronger in many ways, versus negative energy (from emotions such as anger, frustration, and despair) which are often so draining. Some believe these positive energies can even counteract or neutralize negative energies. A second benefit is balance; emotional and professional (Remember: "Take your work seriously and yourself lightly"). Finally, we in the helping professions can better achieve and maintain detachment from the situations we work in every day, yet still possess empathy and compassion.

Laughter, like crying, is the body's natural response to stress. It is a built-in coping mechanism. It provides both psychological, physiological, and emotional relief. Humor has the ability to diffuse negative emotions such as anger, tension, frustration, and panic through positive biochemical changes in the body. This natural benefit has been shunned and neglected, even forbidden, because our work, and our workplace, is a serious business—no laughing matter. Humor has not been sanctioned, permitted, or approved by the system! In most work situations, if employees can see the humor (sometimes absurdity) in a situation, they feel they can survive almost anything. Humor, then, can enhance one's ability to function, improve productivity, and even prevent burnout.

## 10.  Improved Instruction

The correct use of humor can facilitate learning and help change peoples' behavior. Humor can give additional insight in communicating ideas. The role of humor in the teaching and learning process is indeed a curious one. It is complex, sometimes confusing, and rarely a laughing matter. Having said this, it must also be stated that one of the most important qualities of good teachers is their use of appropriate humor. The reasons for employing it are many. The most obvious one is that it may keep students attentive because they are never quite sure what is coming next. The real purpose of using appropriate humor in the classroom is to "hook" the students and the teacher, and to link them through enjoyment. As people laugh together, they become one group of human beings enjoying life.

However, there still seems to be a consensus among educators that convergent thinking is heavily emphasized, almost exclusively, in our schools. As discussed previously in sections 7 and 8 of this chapter, the appropriate use of humor in the classroom has the potential to increase divergent thinking, an essential element of creativity.

Shared laughter between and among the teacher and students is a powerful reinforcer of learning. The following are more alleged benefits of intentionally using appropriate humor in the classroom:

◆ Retention of material. Kaplan and Pascoe (1977) state humor can aid in retention of material by developing and promoting the use of cues, a sort of visual mnemonic device. The authors also discovered in their research on the use of humor in the classroom that the retention of concept humor material was improved significantly after watching a lesson employing humorous examples.

◆ Attentiveness and interest. We learn best when in a state of moderate arousal. Humor involves the audience. When the audience, in this case, our students, are attentive and involved, they can learn and their behaviors can change.

  Students are more attentive when humor is employed by the teacher because they are never really sure just what is coming next. Humor can effectively be used to not only obtain a student's attention, but also maintain it. Highet (1963) perhaps said it best; "The wise teacher will continue to introduce flashes of humor extraneously, because he knows that fifty-five minutes of work plus five minutes of laughter are worth twice as much as sixty minutes of unvaried work" (p. 60).

◆ Student-teacher rapport. Humor can be used in a classroom to enhance the atmosphere and general learning environment. Humor employed in this fashion serves as an immediacy behavior, that is, a behavior that decreases the psychological distance between teacher and student. Thus, verbal and nonverbal closeness is increased. This increased closeness has positive effects on both cognitive and affective learning. The student-teacher relationship is also enhanced when the teacher uses humor to reinforce desired behaviors. Remember a time as a student when you received a nod, smile, or wink from a teacher? How did you feel? It is obvious humor is an effective positive reinforcer, especially if you still remember that incident to this day! Hence, humor can occasionally provide a moment of deep, intrapersonal communication between learner and teacher.

I believe most people learn best by the use of carefully selected and relevant examples. I always try to give numerous examples when I am teaching, and often ask students to generate their own examples back to me as a test of their comprehension of the concept or subject matter. Interestingly, it has been my experience that students can sometimes learn a concept more easily when presented a "non-instance," or non-example, of the concept. In other words, by laughing at the "wrong way" to do something, or laughing at an "absurd" or "ridiculous" example related to a particular concept, the student remembers laughing at it at a gut level. This sends up a red flag as students approach the situation again! "This is ridiculous, it won't work!" or "Don't do this, it's the wrong way." The student often remembers the negative consequences associated with the wrong scenario, and therefore there is little chance for confusion. The student then selects the right answer or a more appropriate response.

◆ Making students' learning more enjoyable. The inclusion of humor in academic lessons may improve selective attention to some degree and makes learning more enjoyable. When teachers and administrators say they want to make learning more enjoyable for students, what they really want is to create a good learning environment.

A good classroom environment or a good learning environment can be enhanced through the use of appropriate humor. The proper use of humor may result in numerous benefits to the improvement of school climate, including the promotion of flexibility, greater facilitation of communication, and to some degree, the creation of a feeling of general goodwill. It would seem the use of appropriate humor in the classroom can lead to a positive classroom climate and more enjoyable learning for students.

To best summarize this section, we should remember the teacher is the key to any laughter and joy that occurs in the classroom. The teacher must be able to find humor in the moment-to-moment or day-to-day interactions with students even when numerous frustrations occur in the classroom. The teacher must show their joy of teaching, for it is the teacher who is the model of a happy, caring person in the student's eyes.

# 11. Tension Release

We live in an increasingly complex society. Humor can be a great remedy for stress and tension. When laughter occurs, there is a contraction followed by an immediate release that is mentally and physically beneficial. The equivalent to internal jogging, a good belly laugh exercises and therefore relaxes every major muscle group in the body. Some say laughing at least 100 times a day is the equivalent of ten minutes of rowing. The decision is not a hard one for me to make. Each morning I ask myself, "Ten minutes of rowing or 100 laughs? Ten minutes of rowing or 100 laughs?" What appropriate and adequate substitutes do you prefer for your classroom?

Humor can also relax and engage students resulting in increased motivation and attention. Think about it; humor is both popular and powerful. When people see or hear humor, they almost automatically pay attention to it, both visually and auditorily. A desired increase in productivity and performance are then realized.

Humor has also been effectively used in teaching "taboo" or "highly technical" subject matter. For example, sex education and family values units have been innovatively taught using appropriate humor (Adams, 1974). This author has taught computer skills to everyone from young children through older adults using humor, because a serious and complex subject is made more approachable and "lightened" through the effective use of appropriate and relevant humor. The key is the fact that the "fear of failure" by individuals in the group is reduced, or even eliminated, through shared laughter. I begin computer classes I teach by placing a cartoon on the overhead screen showing a woman kneeling by the bed praying. The caption reads, "And please, Lord, don't let me make a fool of myself tomorrow during that executive hands-on computer class." Upon reading this, the class laughs in unison and most sit back in their chairs more relaxed. They are now released from their "mental chains" of preconceived fear and apprehension (resulting in anxiety and stress) and are ready to learn. Humor helps people feel less threatened or embarrassed by the prospect of change.

# 12. Relief from Boredom

Mediocrity is often caused by boredom as much as anything else. Boredom can also cause absenteeism and low morale. Humor can go a long way to maintain attention and provide a fresh and much needed infusion of energy into the learning process!

We live with the idea of compulsory attendance; students must attend our classrooms. If teachers are not interesting, students rapidly become uninterested. If we bore our learners, we become baby-sitters and custodians rather than teachers.

Teachers can use enthusiasm and humor to foster the joy and discovery of learning in students of all ages. This is perhaps the real responsibility of a teacher. To do less would be a great disservice!

## Summary

In conclusion, I offer the following. The use of appropriate humor in the classroom results in numerous and varied benefits. Instead of detracting from the educational experience, instructional humor seems to enhance the teaching and learning process. Appropriate and frequent classroom laughter may serve to promote the retention of academic material, reduce academic anxiety in learning and testing situations, liberate thinking, and perhaps most importantly, increase learner satisfaction with the entire experience.

# 11 How to Develop Your Sense of Humor, or "You Say You Don't Think You're Very Funny"

Do any of the following statements apply to you?

◆ I often laugh when others are laughing, only to realize several minutes later I had no idea what was so funny.

◆ I usually can find some humor in most situations.

◆ I think I don't have a sense of humor because I can never remember a joke.

◆ I often laugh at things others don't seem to find funny.

◆ Sometimes I find myself laughing at inappropriate times and in inappropriate places.

◆ Many times when someone tells a story or joke that others find funny, I don't "get" it.

◆ I often think life would be easier for me if I had a better sense of humor.

◆ I'm sometimes afraid to use humor in my classroom because I feel I might lose control to the point of total chaos.

◆ I usually laugh when others say or do something funny, but I rarely initiate any humor.

◆ I find it easy to laugh at myself.

◆ I think I take myself too seriously most of the time.

◆ I can remember jokes, but I'm just no good at telling jokes.

If any of these sound familiar, then this chapter is for you. Why do we laugh at the things we do? Is laughter really contagious? What is the origin of laughter and humor? Why do we laugh when we do? Why do some people find a joke or story funny, while others do not? These questions will be addressed in this chapter as we explore the nature of one's sense of humor.

The ability to laugh is said to distinguish humans from other animals. It has often been said someone can teach you about comedy, but no one can teach you how to be funny. You either have a good sense of humor or you do not. People have believed this for years. I offer a different perspective. I believe that we all have a potential for laughter and a more expanded sense of humor.

## The Development of Humor

Humor is developmental. Therefore, it changes through the years. The sense of humor of a 5-year-old is markedly different than that of a 13-year-old. Adolescent humor is different from adult humor. This is why young children love jokes that adults find extremely silly, and why adolescents often engage in crude or raw humor that adults sometimes find coarse, vulgar, or unrefined.

Although each individual's sense of humor is unique, there are certain developmental patterns applicable to most of us. These patterns seem to parallel an individual's emotional, linguistic, and intellectual development. As I present the developmental sequence of humor, please refrain from acting upon an impulse to seriously compare your own sense of humor to the following chart and act like parents with a 10-month-old in a doctor's office! This represents a general progression of development, combined and collected from a variety of sources (McGhee, 1983; Mindess et al., 1982; Mosak, 1987). Don't use this as a point of reference. It is meant to demonstrate that we all do have a sense of humor. As mentioned previously, numerous variables affect the formation of a sense of humor.

It appears that each human being is born with the potential for the development of a sense of humor. Because each individual is unique, each individual's sense of humor is somewhat different. It is important to note here that the content of a person's experiences is shaped by parents, family, and peers. This shaping occurs in the social, community, and school environments. It seems only natural a person's sense of humor is also shaped by these environments.

A sense of humor is multidimensional, involving the elements (and accompanying ability levels) of identification, appreciation, mirth response, comprehension, and production. Through the practice of certain skills and techniques, I believe that the elements of humor can be taught. With awareness and practice, one's existing sense of humor can be further developed, and its multidimensionality enhanced.

| AGE | | BEHAVIORS |
| --- | --- | --- |
| Week 1 | : | Smiles during sleep. |
| | | Smiles as response to tactile stimulation. |
| 2 Months | : | Grins at discovery of a human face and funny faces. |
| 4 Months | : | Laughs at tickling. Laughs during teasing, peekaboo games, and play with large, colorful toys. |
| 2–4 Years | : | Rhyming and nonsense words are funny; nonsense verses, practical jokes, their own mistakes, general silliness are the source of laughter. |
| 4–6 Years | : | Laughs at any or all of the following: slapstick, misnaming people or objects, silly rhyming, body functions and noises, taboo words, clowning around. Enjoys simple riddles. Appreciates humor to the point of beginning to try to produce humor (creating jokes and riddles). Surprises and exaggerations are also funny. |
| 7–8 Years | : | Aware of increased linguistic ability resulting in ambiguity. At this stage, humor is often couched in taking things literally. Example: The teacher says, "Please take a seat." The student responds, "Where do you want me to take it?" Practical jokes are very common. The plight of discomfort of others is thought to be very funny. Jokes (especially knock-knock jokes) and riddles overheard are repeated again and again. |
| 9–12 Years | : | Jokes, riddles, puns, and other forms of wordplay are common. Anything deviating from the norm is perceived as very funny, such as the use of taboo words or subjects in riddles or jokes, increased linguistic ability results in a marked increase in the use of verbal humor and teasing and in the acceptance of self-ridicule and self-disparaging remarks. |
| 13 Years+ | : | Begins to reflect on the "whys" of humor. More advanced forms of humor employed, such as sarcasm, social and political satire, puns, irony, parody, and other forms of verbal wit. |

## Developing Your Personal Sense of Humor

Most people agree that humor is a highly personal and very subjective form of human expression. This is why people differ so in their reactions to certain forms of humor and why we have preferences for different types of humor. Personality traits are indeed a major factor. A question remains: "If you believe humor can be taught, how can cultivating your sense of humor best be accomplished?" I suggest the following premises:

◆ You do have a sense of humor.

◆ How you use it and how frequently you use it are expressions of your personality.

◆ What you find funny distinguishes you from others.

◆ The expression of your sense of humor may vary from situation to situation.

This book illustrates how you can intentionally and effectively infuse appropriate humor into your classroom. A side-benefit of doing so may be an increase in your own personal sense of humor. However, I believe that humor (as with thinking or creativity) is not an innate attribute with a given quantity or quality, but rather is a *skill* that can be developed with practice.

You can change your sense of humor, if you are willing to take the risk. There is no such thing as a "good" or "bad" sense of humor. You can work hard to rediscover your sense of humor, redefine it, enhance it, and practice it, just as you can learn at any age to manage your anger, learn a foreign language, or learn to play a musical instrument. Following are 10 ways that you can begin to develop or continue to develop your personal sense of humor (and take yourself lightly).

## Top 10 Ways to Develop Your Personal Sense of Humor

1. Begin to purchase, collect, and read a wide variety of humorous material. I suggest reading something as soon as you wake up in the morning, and let it be one of the last things you do at night. You might begin with some of the resources listed in the back matter. Public and school libraries are perhaps the most convenient sources for material.

2. Rent or purchase video tapes of some of your favorite comedies. I have many videotapes of television comedies I personally find hilarious. I can then watch them over and

over again, whenever I want. My video library includes: *The Honeymooners*, *I Love Lucy*, *Monty Python's Flying Circus*, and *Are You Being Served?*, to name a few. Stores often carry collections of these popular television shows. Renting comedy videos of recent movies and classics is also beneficial.

3. Lighten up! Try being a bit more playful, dramatic, or silly. Others may pick up on your laughter and sense of humor. Begin experimenting with humor with one close friend and then expand to others. Eventually, you might try some of this appropriate humor in your work setting, at an informal social gathering, or even in your classroom.

4. Smile more! It is simple, and people who smile are better liked! It has been said it takes 27 muscles to frown and only 3 to smile!

5. Recall personally humorous stories from your own life experiences. These are the material for anecdotes you can use in numerous situations with people.

6. Try to find "fixed" times you can share humor with family members, coworkers, and your students. At home, try watching situation comedies together or telling jokes at the dinner table. During dinner at our house, each member of the family must tell the funniest thing that happened at school or work that day. At work, share humorous anecdotes from the classroom that day with colleagues, in the hall or in the teacher's lounge.

7. Carry some appropriate humor with you at all times in your wallet or purse and be prepared to share it with others.

8. Many adults have developed FOLF Syndrome—Fear Of Looking Foolish. We often refrain from using our imagination, creativity, and even risk-taking behaviors because of this syndrome. Try to infuse humor in a variety of "serious" situations.

9. Conducting an activity at home or in the classroom just for the fun of it is also a beneficial exercise. Teachers are often so busy developing, implementing, and evaluating instructional objectives, course outlines, and curricula materials that they often do not take time to notice or become involved in the fun, enjoyment, and sheer excitement of teaching and learning.

10. Occasionally, sprinkle internal professional correspondence or personal correspondence with humor. Remember, as the advertising profession has known for decades, humor sells.

The various types and categories of humor presented here are obviously not for every teacher. However, for those who generally feel comfortable using some humor throughout the learning process in the classroom, this book provides suggestions and guidelines for its use, as we all try to make teaching and learning more successful and enjoyable.

## Humor in Your Daily Life

Humor is a substantial and significant part of our daily lives. In our society, possessing a good sense of humor is highly valued. Very few people would admit to not having a sense of humor. We may gain a great deal of pleasure and gratification by being the source of humor-arousal for others. Although most of us would agree with the previous statement, more often we find ourselves in the role of the "straight-man" instead of having the reputation of "comedian." However, most would agree that a good sense of humor is an inestimable asset in almost any personal, professional, or social situation.

I believe that a differentiation must be made here between "joking" and a "sense of humor." Joking is something done in deliberate fashion to cause laughter. A sense of humor is generally thought of as something someone has that encompasses joking. Joking, then, is only one small part of a total sense of humor. Our sense of humor involves both the ability to amuse others and the readiness to laugh as the recipient of the humor. Both of these actions may or may not involve joking. However, both joking and the sense of humor involve mirth and laughter.

## Summary

A further note: I have been discussing your individual sense of humor as if it is something that can be enhanced or developed in isolation. Remember, laughter is a social phenomenon. You cannot tell a joke to make yourself laugh. You cannot tickle yourself to make yourself laugh. Laughter is for sharing with others. Laughter is also contagious.

So, after reading this chapter, you still may say one of the following:

◆ I just can't tell a joke.

◆ I don't remember jokes.

◆ I don't find funny the type of jokes or stories my friends like.

◆ I'm just not a humorous person.

◆ I don't have a good sense of humor.

Remember, there is more to the development of a sense of humor than being able to tell a joke. As this book has demonstrated, humor is comprised of five elements: identification, appreciation, mirth response, comprehension, and production. A sense of humor involves all of these elements in varying degrees. Perhaps you identify and comprehend a particular joke, yet you do not appreciate that kind of humor and do not laugh at it. Perhaps you appreciate satire when you hear it, but you cannot produce humor when asked to do so. The production of humor often requires the development of various and numerous skills such as timing and constructing a set-up and a punch line. You must enjoy the accompanying sense of power that comes from knowing you have inspired others to laugh, and you must feel comfortable being the center of attention.

Other variables or factors include sociological ones, such as the members of the group in which the humor is being relayed, age, gender, audience feedback, and mirth response. Your sense of humor may be well-developed in one or two of these areas and not the others. This is perfectly normal!

# Appendix
## Humor Action Plan

NAME: _____

ADDRESS: _____

PHONE: _____

TITLE (Be complete and descriptive) _____

_____

_____

_____

_____

GOALS/OBJECTIVES/OUTCOMES:

Continues on page 118.

**BRIEF DESCRIPTION OF PLAN AND HOW YOU WILL IMPLEMENT:**

**FORMAL/INFORMAL METHODS OF MEASURING RESULTS:**

**TENTATIVE TIMELINE:** _____

# References

Adams, W. 1974. The use of sexual humor in teaching human sexuality at the university level. *Family Coordinator* 23:365–68.

Bergson, H. 1911. *Laughter: An essay on the meaning of the comic.* New York: Macmillan.

Carroll, L. 1960. *Alices' adventures in wonderland.* New York: Signet.

Cousins, N. 1981. *Anatomy of an illness.* New York: Bantam Books.

Darwin, C. 1965. *The expression of emotions in man and animals.* Chicago: University of Chicago Press.

Eastman, M. 1936. *Enjoyment of laughter.* New York: Simon and Schuster.

Fabrizi, M., and H. Pollio. 1987. A naturalistic study of humorous activity in a third, seventh, and eleventh grade classroom. *Merrill-Palmer Quarterly* 33 (1):107–28.

Gagne, A. 1970. *The conditions of learning.* New York: Holt, Rinehart, and Winston.

Herbert, B. 1981. *Classic comebacks.* Los Angeles: Price, Stern, and Sloan.

Highet, G. 1963. *The art of teaching.* New York: Knopf.

Johnson, M. 1976. I think my teacher is a. . . . *Learning* 4:36–38.

Kaplan, R., and G. Pascoe. 1977. Humorous lectures and humorous examples: Some effects upon comprehension and retention. *Journal of Educational Psychology* 69:61–65.

Larson, G. *The Far Side gallery series.* Kansas City: Universal Press Syndicate.

Lederer, R. 1987. *Anguished English: An anthology of accidental assaults upon our language.* Charleston, NC: Wyrick and Company.

Marshall, J. 1989. *The cut-ups at Camp Custer.* New York: Viking Kestrel.

Marshall, J. 1992. *The cut-ups crack up.* New York: Viking Penguin.

Masten, A. 1986. Humor and competence in school-aged children. *Child Development* 57:461–73.

McGhee, P. 1983. The role of arousal and hemispheric lateralization in humor. In *Handbook of humor research: Basic issues,* P. E. McGhee and J. H. Goldstein, eds. New York: Springer-Verlag.

Mindess, H., et al. 1982. *The Antioch humor test: Making sense of humor.* New York: Argon Books.

Mosak, H. 1987. *Ha ha and aha: The role of humor in psychotherapy.* Muncie, IN: Accelerated Development, Inc.

Prelutsky, J. 1991. *For laughing out loud: Poems to tickle your funny bone.* New York: Knopf.

Prelutsky, J. 1993. *Nonny Mouse writes again.* New York: Knopf.

Prelutsky, J. 1990. *Something big has been here.* New York: Greenwillow Books.

Schacht, S., and B. Stewart. 1990. What's funny about statistics? A technique for reducing student anxiety. *Teaching Sociology* 18:52–56.

Shade, R. (in press) Figural humor (cartoons) as an alternative assessment.

Shade, R. 1991. Verbal humor in gifted students and students in the general population: A comparison of spontaneous mirth response and comprehension. *Journal for the Education of the Gifted* 14 (2):134–50.

Shepherd, C., J. Kohut, and R. Sweet. 1990. *More news of the weird.* New York: Plume.

Silverstein, S. 1981. *A light in the attic.* New York: Harper and Row.

Silverstein, S. 1974. *Where the sidewalk ends.* New York: Harper and Row.

White, E. B. 1953. Remarks on humor in *The second tree from the corner.* New York: Harper and Row.

Wiseman, B. 1989. *Morris the Moose*. New York: Harper and Row.

Wiseman, B. 1970. *Morris the Moose goes to school*. New York: Scholastic.

Zigler, E., J. Levine, and L. Gould. 1967. Cognitive challenge as a factor in children's humor appreciation. *Journal of Personality and Social Psychology* 6:332–36.

Zigler, E., J. Levine, and L. Gould. 1966. Cognitive processes in the development of children's appreciation of humor. *Child Development* 37, 507-518.

## Additional Reference Books

Bleedorn, B., and S. McKelvey. *HUMOR: Lessons in laughter for learning and living*. Buffalo, NY: D.O.K. Publishers, 1986.

Carter, Judy. *Stand-up comedy: The book*. New York: Dell Publishing Group, 1989.

Cousins, Norman. 1979. *Anatomy of an illness*. New York: Bantam Books.

Garland, R. 1991. *Making work fun: Doing business with a sense of humor*. San Diego, CA: Shamrock Press.

Hoomes, E. 1987. *Laughing matters*. Hawthorne, NJ: Educational Impressions.

Kelly, W. 1988. *Laughter & learning*. Portland, MA: J. Weston Walch.

Loomans, D., and K. Kolberg. 1993. *The laughing classroom: Everyone's guide to teaching with humor and play*. Tiburon, CA: H. J. Kramer, Inc.

McGhee, Paul, and J. Goldstein. 1983. *Handbook of humor research*. New York: Springer-Verlag.

Metcalf, C., and R. Felible. 1992. *Lighten up: Survival skills for people under pressure*. Reading, MA: Addison-Wesley.

Williamson, ˊB. 1993. *Playful activities for powerful presentations*. Duluth, MN: Whole Person Associates, Inc.

## Humor Journals

*International Journal of Humor Research*

| **For North America:** | **For all other countries:** |
|---|---|
| Walter de Gruyter, Inc. | Walter de Gruyter & Co. |
| 200 Saw Mill River Road | Postfach 30 34 21 |
| Hawthorne, NY 10532 | D-10728 Berlin |
| USA | Federal Republic of Germany |

## Laughing Matters

The HUMOR Project
110 Spring Street
Saratoga Springs, NY 12866

## Kits

*Blitz Cartoon Kit*

Can be ordered from:
Blitz Art Products, Inc.
P.O. Box 8022
Cherry Hill, NJ 08002

Includes the book:
   Blitz, B. 1991. *How to draw Blitz cartoons.* Philadelphia:
   Running Press.

# Index

# About the Author

Dr. Shade lives and works in Laramie, Wyoming, where he is an Associate Professor of Special Education at the University of Wyoming. He teaches courses in gifted and talented, special education, and humor. Before moving to university teaching, Dr. Shade taught both elementary and secondary gifted and talented students in Pennsylvania public schools.

In addition to university teaching, Dr. Shade presents nationally at professional conferences. He has published numerous articles related to humor in education, as well as other special education issues, in professional journals. For the past six years, he has conducted a three-week humor workshop for talented youth at the University of Wyoming's High School Summer Institute.

Dr. Shade's work with humor is well-known by teachers and administrators in the field. He has presented to a variety of school groups, organizations, and school districts. His workshops in humor are in demand, and are described by participants as "fast-paced, fun, practical, and a laugh a minute!"